The Chihuahua

OUR BEST FRIENDS

OUR BEST FRIENDS

The Chihuahua

Elaine Waldorf Gewirtz

ELDORADO INK

Produced by OTTN Publishing, Stockton, New Jersey

Eldorado Ink
PO Box 100097
Pittsburgh, PA 15233
www.eldoradoink.com

CPSIA compliance information: Batch#OBF010111-3. For further information,
contact Eldorado Ink at info@eldoradoink.com.

First printing

1 3 5 7 9 8 6 4 2

Library of Congress Cataloging-in-Publication Data

Gewirtz, Elaine Waldorf.
  The Chihuahua / Elaine Waldorf Gewirtz.
      p. cm. — (Our best friends)
  Includes bibliographical references and index.
  ISBN 978-1-932904-75-8 (hardcover) — ISBN 978-1-932904-81-9 (trade)
  1. Chihuahua (Dog breed) I. Title.
  SF429.C45G493 2011
  636.76—dc22

                            2010034488

**For information about custom editions, special sales, or premiums,
please contact our special sales department at info@eldoradoink.com.**

TABLE OF CONTENTS

Introduction

GARY KORSGAARD, DVM

The mutually beneficial relationship between humans and animals began long before the dawn of recorded history. Archaeologists believe that humans began to capture and tame wild goats, sheep, and pigs more than 9,000 years ago. These animals were then bred for specific purposes, such as providing humans with a reliable source of food or providing furs and hides that could be used for clothing or the construction of dwellings.

Other animals had been sought for companionship and assistance even earlier. The dog, believed to be the first animal domesticated, began living and working with Stone Age humans in Europe more than 14,000 years ago. Some archaeologists believe that wild dogs and humans were drawn together because both hunted the same prey. By taming and training dogs, humans became more effective hunters. Dogs, meanwhile, enjoyed the social contact with humans and benefited from greater access to food and warm shelter. Dogs soon became beloved pets as well as trusted workers. This can be seen from the many artifacts depicting dogs that have been found at ancient sites in Asia, Europe, North America, and the Middle East.

The earliest domestic cats appeared in the Middle East about 5,000 years ago. Small wild cats were probably first attracted to human settlements because plenty of rodents could be found wherever harvested grain was stored. Cats played a useful role in hunting and killing these pests, and it is likely that grateful humans rewarded them for this assistance. Over time, these small cats gave up some of their aggressive wild behaviors and began living among humans. Cats eventually became so popular in ancient Egypt that they were believed to possess magical powers. Cat statues were placed outside homes to ward off evil spirits, and mummified cats were included in royal tombs to accompany their owners into the afterlife.

Today, few people believe that cats have supernatural powers, but most pet owners feel a magical bond with their pets, whether they are dogs, cats, hamsters, rabbits, horses, or parrots. The lives of pets and their people become inextricably intertwined, providing strong emotional and physical rewards for both humans and animals. People of all ages can benefit from the loving companionship of a pet. Not surprisingly, then, pet ownership is widespread. Recent statistics indicate that about 60 percent of all households in the United States and Canada have at least one pet, while the figure is close to 50 percent of households in the United Kingdom. For millions of people, therefore, pets truly have become their "best friends."

Finding the best animal friend can be a challenge, however. Not only are there many types of domesticated pets, but each has specific needs, characteristics, and personality traits. Even within a category of pets, such as dogs, different breeds will flourish in different surroundings and with different treatment. For example, a German Shepherd may not be the right pet for a person living in a cramped urban apartment; that person might be better off caring for a smaller dog like a Toy Poodle or Shih Tzu, or perhaps a cat. On the other hand, an active person who loves the outdoors may prefer the companion-ship of a Labrador Retriever to that of a small dog or a passive indoor pet like a goldfish or hamster.

The joys of pet ownership come with certain responsibilities. Bringing a pet into your home and your neighborhood obligates you to care for and train the pet properly. For example, a dog must be housebroken, taught to obey your commands, and trained to behave appropriately when he encounters other people or animals. Owners must also be mindful of their pet's particular nutritional and medical needs.

The purpose of the OUR BEST FRIENDS series is to provide a helpful and comprehensive introduction to pet ownership. Each book contains the basic information a prospective pet owner needs in order to choose the right pet for his or her situation and to care for that pet throughout the pet's lifetime. Training, socialization, proper nutrition, potential medical issues, and the legal responsibilities of pet ownership are thoroughly explained and discussed, and an abundance of expert tips and suggestions are offered. Whether it is a hamster, corn snake, guinea pig, or Labrador Retriever, the books in the OUR BEST FRIENDS series provide everything the reader needs to know about how to have a happy, well-adjusted, and well-behaved pet.

Chihuahuas, the smallest dog breed, are intelligent, alert, and graceful dogs. Because of their small size, they take up little room, making them excellent apartment dwellers.

CHAPTER ONE

Is a Chihuahua Right for You?

The Chihuahua, with his sweet intelligent nature, is one of the most popular dog breeds in the United States. Chihuahuas are graceful, alert, and small enough to tote on your arm. Don't underestimate this sharp-eared watchdog, though: a Chihuahua won't hesitate to use his unmistakable shrill bark to protect his territory. His Napoleonic personality mixes extreme sensitivity with big-dog posturing, all wrapped in a neat and tidy six-pound package.

Bringing a Chihuahua into your household can be great fun, but the decision to add a pet to your family should never be taken lightly. A companionable dog such as a Chihuahua requires a lengthy commitment, because these dogs typically live 12 to 15 years or more. You'll need to properly train and socialize your Chihuahua so he won't grow into an obnoxious barker with a snappish temperament. You'll need to protect him from larger, more aggressive dogs, as well as from young children who may want to treat him roughly. You'll have to provide health care, ensure that he receives proper nutrition, pay attention to his appearance, and make sure that he gets enough exercise. All of these responsibilities take time and effort, so make sure that you're ready before bringing a Chihuahua home.

To get an idea of what living with this diminutive breed is like, talk with other Chihuahua owners if you have an opportunity. Chances are, you'll hear about the following attributes of this breed:

SMALL STATURE: The tiniest of the toy breeds, the typical Chihuahua stands 6 to 9 inches (15 to 23 cm) tall when measured from the ground to the top of his shoulders. In the show ring Chihuahuas can weigh no more than 6 pounds (2.7 kg). Larger Chihuahuas make wonderful pets, too, but tiny Chihuahuas weighing less than 3 pounds (1.4 kg) are more susceptible to medical problems. Because of their small stature, this breed is popular with people who live in apartments or smaller homes.

LOVES PAMPERING: If you enjoy spoiling a small dog with attention, a Chihuahua might be the right pet for you. Chihuahuas love oversized beds and pillows. These dogs won't mind traveling with you in a shoulder bag, or being dressed up in tiny sweaters, coats, canine jewelry, and fancy collars.

SMALL GUARD DOGS: Despite their small size, Chihuahuas naturally have watchdog tendencies. A protective breed, they will let out a series of sharp, ear-splitting barks when someone comes to the door or they hear an unusual noise. Chihuahuas are not comfortable with strangers; they will bark or growl if one approaches, and will place themselves between their owners and the newcomer.

Smooth coated Chihuahuas need very little grooming due to their short hair. Long coats need occasional brushing but still require minimal grooming.

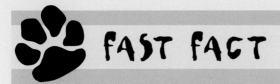

LITTLE GROOMING REQUIRED: Compared to other dogs, the Chihuahua is a low-maintenance breed. However, Chihuahuas still need a monthly bath; regular brushing, nail trimming, and ear cleaning; and daily dental brushing.

EASY TO TRAIN: Chihuahuas need proper training so that they don't get the idea that they're in charge of the household. Fortunately, these dogs are smart and want to please their owners, so they can learn relatively quickly to follow your commands. It's definitely easier to control a six-pound dog than it is to control a larger dog, but you'll still need to use firm commands and demonstrate your authority during training sessions.

INTERACTING WITH OTHERS

As a small dog, a Chihuahua may seem like the perfect companion for a small child. However, this delicate breed requires patience and gentle handling. If a wobbly toddler falls on a Chihuahua or a young child picks one up and accidentally drops him, your dog can become seriously injured. Unexpected juvenile screams or sudden movements will scare a Chihuahua and might cause him to react aggressively. Chihuahuas are intelligent, and they won't forget a bad experience with a child. This could lead them to growl, snap, or possibly bite a child the next time they encounter one. If there are children in your home, they must be taught how to handle and play with a Chihuahua correctly. For everyone's safety, all interactions between kids and dogs require adult supervision.

Before bringing a Chihuahua into the household, consider how other animals in the family may react. If you already have a big dog, adding a Chihuahua will require separation or constant supervision in order to prevent rough play or squabbling. Large dogs with a

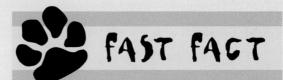

strong drive to chase and kill small animals may view your Chihuahua as prey, not as a fellow pet. Compounding this problem, Chihuahuas are very protective of "their" territory and will not back down from a dog many times their size. You'll always need to protect your little dog from danger.

ORIGIN OF THE CHIHUAHUA

The origins of this diminutive breed are unknown. One of the forebears of the modern Chihuahua may have been a small dog called the Techichi, which was first domesticated by the Toltec Indians of Mesoamerica (Mexico and part of Central America) more than a thousand years ago. The Toltecs kept the dogs as pets, employed them for hunting small game, and also used them in religious ceremonies. Techichi dogs were larger than modern Chihuahuas; they also were mute and longhaired. Remains of these dogs have been found in human graves, as well as in the pyramid-temples at Cholula and Chichén Itzá.

Remains of Techichi dogs have been found in ancient Mesoamerican temples, such as the complex at Chichén Itzá.

The Chihuahua is named after the Mexican state of Chihuahua; the word is derived from the Nahuati word *Xicuahua*, which means "dry, sandy place." (Inset) Novelist Owen Wister (1860-1938) helped to popularize the Chihuahua in America during the late 19th century.

When the Aztecs emerged as rulers of Mesoamerica during the 14th century, they embraced many aspects of Toltec culture. The Aztecs adopted Techichi dogs as pets, incorporated them into sacred rituals, and sometimes used them for food.

The Chihuahua breed may have developed as a result of crossbreeding between Techichi dogs and small terrier-type dogs from Malta. These dogs would have been brought to the New World by the Spanish conquistadors who defeated and subjugated the Aztecs during the 16th century. Techichi may also have been bred with small, hairless dogs from Asia. No one knows for certain, as practically no information about these dogs exists from the time of the Spanish conquest in the 1520s until the mid-19th century. In whatever way the crossbreeding occurred, the resulting Chihuahua dogs grew smaller and louder than their Techichi ancestors.

The modern dog breed takes its name from the Mexican state of Chihuahua, where the earliest specimens of the breed were found. Chihuahua is located in northwestern Mexico, and borders the U.S. states Texas and New Mexico. In the mid- to late-19th century, American tourists visiting the Chihuahua region became interested in the small dog. They started bringing them back to their homes as souvenirs, calling them Mexican Chihuahuas. (In Mexico, the breed is called Chihuahueno.)

During the 1890s, Philadelphia novelist Owen Wister returned from a visit to Texas with several of these small dogs. He and his friend Charles Stewart established one of the first Chihuahua breeding programs. Other American breeders also began concentrating on producing Chihuahuas around this time. The first breed registry, or "stud book"—an official list of pedigreed animals within a specific breed—was created by the late 1890s. The American Kennel Club officially recognized the Chihuahua breed in 1904. That year, the AKC registered its first Chihuahua: Midget, owned by H. Raynor of El Paso, Texas. In 1923, Chihuahua fanciers and breeders who wanted to set the standards by which their favorite little dogs would be judged formed the Chihuahua Club of America.

THE IDEAL CHIHUAHUA

It's no accident that purebred Chihuahuas today look pretty much the same as they did when the American Kennel Club first recognized the breed more than a century ago. Breeders aim to produce dogs that closely match a description of

WHAT IS A MOLERA?

One thing that is unique about the Chihuahua is that these dogs are born with a skin-covered opening in their skulls called a molera. This opening, which is also called a fontanel, is similar to the soft spot in a human baby's skull. The reason for the molera is to allow a Chihuahua pup's head to pass through the mother's birth canal during delivery. You can detect a molera by gently pressing on the skin in the middle of the skull. If the skin gives slightly, you've felt the molera.

The soft spot is usually about the size of a dime.

A molera won't affect a Chihuahua's activity level and doesn't require veterinary attention or treatment. The molera usually shrinks as a dog ages, but sometimes it stays open throughout the Chihuahua's life. If your Chihuahua has a molera that remains open, take special care to avoid head injuries, as serious brain damage can occur because of the soft spot.

the ideal Chihuahua's appearance and temperament. This description is called the standard of perfection, or the breed standard. Members of the Chihuahua Club of America developed and published the original standard of perfection in 1924, and it has been slightly modified several times since then. This standard, which has been adopted by the American Kennel Club, gives breeders a written description of the attributes that make the Chihuahua unique.

The current Chihuahua breed standard can be found online at www.akc.org/breeds/chihuahua/index.cfm. It describes a graceful and compact dog with a lively and alert expression. The "apple dome" head gives the breed a distinctive appearance. Large, erect ears are set low on the head but carried high to balance out the short, tapered muzzle. Large luminous eyes complete the Chihuahua's watchful expression.

In 1952, the American Kennel Club divided Chihuahuas into two varieties: long coat and smooth coat. The long coat is flat or slightly wavy, while the smooth coat is soft and glossy. On long coat Chihuahuas, longer hair on the feet looks almost like feathers. Long hair on a Chihuahua's legs is referred to as the "pants"; long hair on the chest beneath the neck and stomach is

Purebred Chihuahuas come in two coat varieties: long coat (top) and smooth coat (bottom).

For either type of Chihuahua coat, many colors and patterns are available. Some popular colors include tricolor (black and tan with white markings, left); fawn and white (below); and brown and white (opposite page).

called the "frill." For either type of Chihuahua coat, a wide variety of colors and patterns are available: solid colors, marked (white areas on colored background), or splashed (irregularly patched color on white or irregularly patched white on color).

According to the breed standard, the ideal Chihuahua has a confident, independent temperament. These dogs are alert, bold, and courageous, and tend to protect their territory. Their keen senses of sight and hearing make members of this vigilant

If you think you'll be irritated by a "clingy" dog, a Chihuahua is probably not right for you. Chihuahuas enjoy being touched, petted, and held. If your Chihuahua thinks he's being ignored, he will try to get your attention in various ways.

breed excellent watchdogs. Chihuahuas enjoy being active, and will eagerly demonstrate their running and leaping ability in competitive sports and games.

While every dog is different, in general Chihuahuas are intelligent and fast learners. Members of this breed tend to establish a strong bond with one member of the family, and it's not unusual for a Chihuahua to follow his chosen person around the house every minute of the day. Some Chihuahuas will even become jealous if another dog wants to share his favorite family member's space. Most important, these dogs love to please their humans. By patiently providing consistent training, you can build a strong relationship with a Chihuahua dog that will last more than a decade.

CHAPTER TWO

Finding the Right Chihuahua

Once you've decided to add a Chihuahua to your life, the next step is finding a healthy, well-adjusted dog. Because Chihuahuas are popular as a breed, puppies and adult dogs are widely available. The place you start depends on what you desire in a dog. Do you want a show-quality Chihuahua, or are you simply looking for a faithful canine companion? Do you want a puppy you can train from the beginning, or would you prefer to rescue an adult dog from an animal shelter? Do you want a male or a female, or is gender unimportant? Answering these questions will make your search easier. Here are some factors to consider

Training a Chihuahua puppy takes time and dedication, but the reward is worth it.

that may help you find the Chihuahua that is a good match for you and your family.

YOUR GOALS: Choosing the right Chihuahua will be easier if you have an idea about what you would like your dog to accomplish. Are you interested in competitive sports, like obedience, agility, flyball, or canine musical freestyle? Would you like to exhibit your dog in conformation shows? Would you like to get involved in pet-assisted therapy, which involves taking your trained Chihuahua to visit people in hospitals and nursing homes? To find a good purebred candidate for any of these pursuits, seek out breeders whose Chihuahuas have excelled in the sports or activities that interest you most.

Good training and the right kind of stimulation can strengthen and enhance a dog's inherited potential, but for him to excel in a particular activity that potential must be present in the first place. You're more likely to find that potential in a pup whose parents and other relatives already demonstrate that ability. If you have a specific sport or activity in mind for a Chihuahua you are considering, but are fairly new to that activity yourself, have someone with experience evaluate the pup or

FAST FACT

Chihuahua litters can range in size from one to four puppies, although most litters consist of just one or two pups. If a smooth coat Chihuahua carries the gene for long coats, it can produce both long-coated and smooth-coated puppies in the same litter when bred to a long coat Chihuahua.

dog before you make your final decision.

PUPPY VERSUS OLDER DOG: Chihuahua puppies are extremely cute, but raising a tiny canine can be a challenge. You'll have to keep a careful eye on a Chihuahua puppy at all times to make sure he doesn't hurt himself or go to the bathroom in the wrong place. Although Chihuahuas are small, they can still destroy your possessions by chewing them apart. On the other hand, watching a puppy play and grow can be very entertaining. A well-bred puppy gives you the chance to train him exactly the way you want, and the bond you'll build with a puppy lasts a lifetime.

If you'd prefer to skip the work involved in raising a puppy, consider adopting an adolescent or adult Chihuahua. Sometimes you can find

Chihuahuas are extremely loyal and tend to form a strong bond with their owners.

an older purebred dog; for example, a breeder may want to find a home for a dog that failed to fulfill his championship potential or one that is retired from the show ring. Another option is adopting a Chihuahua from a shelter or rescue organization. The most common reason dogs are surrendered to shelters is a change in their owners' circumstances, such as a move to a place that doesn't allow pets. However, some dogs end up in shelters because their previous owner could not manage their behavior or temperament. Again, this may be more the fault of the owner than the dog.

One of the advantages to adopting an older dog is that you'll have a better sense of his temperament and full-grown size. An adult dog will already be past the chewing stage, and may already be housebroken and be able to respond to some basic commands. Often, older dogs have been vaccinated and spayed or neutered.

Don't worry that an older dog won't bond with you. Once you begin caring for an adopted Chihuahua, he'll soon realize that you're the best thing that ever happened to him.

MALE VERSUS FEMALE: Another decision you will need to make is whether you want a male or a female Chihuahua. There are some gender-related differences, but overall the differences between male and female Chihuahuas are minor. Either a male or a female can make a wonderful, affectionate pet.

Whatever you decide, choose carefully and avoid buying a

AVOID RARE AND TEACUP DOGS

Some unscrupulous breeders advertise Teacup, Pocket, or Miniature Chihuahuas for sale and promise that these pups will weigh less than two pounds when full grown. Don't believe these claims—and don't even think of paying a higher price for one of these pups.

Chihuahuas are so tiny as puppies that it's nearly impossible to accurately predict how large they will get as adults. There is no such thing as an "extra-small" size Chihuahua. Smaller pups are normal Chihuahua puppies, not some exotic variation of the breed.

Although the AKC's breed standard establishes that Chihuahuas should weigh less than six pounds, any adult Chihuahua smaller than three pounds is likely to suf-

fer from health problems. Some extremely tiny pups may not be fully developed and are more likely to suffer from heart or lung problems, luxated patellas (slipped kneecaps), or hydrocephalus, which occurs when fluid builds up around the brain.

There's also no such thing as a "rare" colored Chihuahua. The AKC breed standard specifically says that any color is acceptable, so you'll find Chihuahuas in many different solid colors or color combinations. Breeders who advertise "rare" colors or promote their dogs with descriptive names like "Platinum Chihuahuas" or "Velveteen Chihuahuas" are simply trying to trick uneducated customers into paying extra for their puppies.

Chihuahua impulsively. While you can fall in love with any Chihuahua, you're going to live with your choice for a dozen years or more. Take the time necessary to select a healthy, well-adjusted canine companion that is right for you.

CHOOSING A BREEDER

If you decide that you'd like a pure-bred Chihuahua puppy, the next step is to find a reputable breeder. Look for a breeder who is a member of the Chihuahua Club of America, as this separates serious breeders who care about the future of the Chihuahua breed from those who raise puppies purely for profit. CCA members agree to follow a code of ethics that requires them to adhere to strict guidelines with regard to breeding and selling Chihuahua puppies.

Depending on where you live, you might have to drive many hours to reach the nearest Chihuahua Club of America breeder. If that's not practical, you're not necessarily out of luck. Ask a local veterinarian, or friends who own Chihuahuas, for breeder recommendations. You might also attend a dog show, which can be a great place to meet breeders as well as to learn more about the Chihuahua breed.

It's hard to overstate the importance of finding a reputable breeder if you are getting a puppy, especially if you've never owned a Chihuahua before. When you buy a puppy, you're also buying the breeder's

There are only minor differences between male and female Chihuahuas in terms of temperament and activity level. Chihuahuas of either gender can make great pets.

A good way to find the dog of your dreams is to start at the Chihuahua Club of America's Web site, www.chihuahuaclubofamerica.com. Under the "Membership" tab, you'll find a state-by-state directory of Chihuahua breeders. There's also a list of regional Chihuahua clubs throughout the United States. Each of these clubs provides links to reputable breeders, as well as local breed rescues where older Chihuahuas can be found. You can email or telephone the breeders or rescue organizations to learn more about upcoming litters or to add your name to a list of people waiting for older dogs.

expertise. This person should be able to share the latest information about Chihuahua behavior, care, health, and training throughout the dog's life. Look for a breeder who performs health tests on her stock before breeding to make sure they are free from genetic illnesses, such as heart problems and slipped kneecaps. A good breeder can provide a four-generation pedigree for her puppies and can provide details about the appearance, temperament, and health history of all the dogs in that pedigree. Also, conscientious breeders properly socialize their puppies during the first few weeks of their lives by acclimating them to a variety of new sights and sounds. This gives pups confidence, making them less likely to become overly territorial, fearful, or aggressive.

Finding the ideal Chihuahua often requires several hours searching the Internet, then talking on the phone with breeders. Once you've narrowed down your choices, plan to visit the breeders that you like. You'll have a chance to see the breeder's operation and ask questions about their Chihuahuas. Don't expect to buy a puppy on the day you visit, though. The best breeders plan their litters months in advance and only breed a few times each year. Often they have a long waiting list.

When you visit the breeder, look at the conditions in which the puppy has been raised. The kennel area should be clean and well maintained, without food or feces lying around. The pups should have a bowl of fresh water, a few interesting toys, and clean bedding.

Ask to meet the parents. Your puppy will grow up to look and act like the sire and dam, so if you like the parents, chances are you'll love the puppy. Just don't expect adult Chihuahuas to behave like over-friendly Golden Retrievers. Even well bred, good-natured Chihuahuas do not greet strangers exuberantly. They should, however, allow you to see them on a grooming table in a controlled situation. Although they may bark at you from a distance they should never try to bite.

During your visit, expect the breeder to interview you. A good

BUYER BEWARE

You're going to have your Chihuahua for many years, so spend the time it takes to find the ideal breeder and the perfect puppy. Don't buy a puppy just because you see a cute one for sale in a store or at a swap meet. Also, don't buy a puppy from an out-of-state breeder and have the dog shipped to you, even if the breeder seems friendly and knowledge-able on the phone, has a professional-looking Web site, and offers photos of your puppy.

Without actually seeing the environ-ment in which your puppy was raised, you have no way of knowing whether the conditions were clean or whether the pup was handled and well socialized. Puppies neglected during their first weeks of life typically grow up to be fearful and shy. They also have difficulty with housetrain-ing. A pet store may offer you a 24- or 48-hour health guarantee, but problems frequently crop up after that period. While a distant breeder may offer a com-prehensive health guarantee, you're not likely to ship the dog back if you encounter problems. Always visit the breeder and see the puppies for yourself before agreeing to buy one.

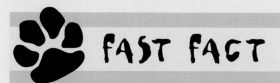 **FAST FACT**

Puppies who are neglected during their first weeks of life grow up fearful and shy. If kept in small cages for long periods, they tend to have difficulty with house-training.

breeder will want to know a bit about you and your family before allowing you to purchase one of her high-quality puppies. She'll probably ask questions about why you want a Chihuahua, your experience with previous dogs, and how you plan to care for your Chihuahua. If she has doubts about your ability to properly train and care for one of her puppies, she won't sell to you.

PICKING A PUPPY

When it is time to select a puppy, you may find that you don't have much of a choice. Chihuahua litters are fairly small, typically from one to four puppies. Sometimes, the breeder will decide to keep one of the puppies for show purposes, or to add a specific color or characteristic to her breeding program.

Before you look at the litters, think about the temperament and personality you'd like in your dog. Puppies are so cute that it's easy to

fall in love with them, but not every pup will be right for you. Handle and observe the pups for a while, then decide whether one is the right animal companion.

You can learn a lot about a puppy by observing him interacting with his siblings. Watch how littermates play, and note which pups act bossy and which get bossed around. One thing you could try is to place a large object, like an open cardboard box, in the puppy play area and watch what they do with it. Some pups will explore it, others may ignore it, and some may wait and watch what the others do, then mimic their actions. This experiment will give you an idea of how each pup approaches unfamiliar situations.

You also want to choose a puppy that is in good health. The puppies should be active and alert, and their eyes and ears must be free from redness or discharge. Their coats should

 **FAST FACT**

A reputable breeder will not let puppies go to their new homes before they are ten to twelve weeks old. Chihuahua puppies need that time with their mother and siblings to learn how to interact with others.

be clean and shiny, and their skin should not have marks or sores. A dull coat and a swollen stomach may indicate parasites. Pups should be able to walk and run without limping. They should also be interested in meeting you, not shying away from your touch. Be on the lookout for an overly large head that seems out of balance with the rest of the body, and eyes that protrude and show too much white at the inside corners. This may indicate hydrocephalus, also known as water on the brain.

THE PROPER PAPERS

An ethical breeder sends a puppy home with a pile of papers. These include an extensive instruction packet filled with information about Chihuahua behavior, care, health and training. You should receive feeding instructions that include the type and amount of food your puppy should eat, and when he should eat it. The breeder will probably discuss these things with you before you pick up the dog, but the paperwork can help answer questions after you get home.

On the day you take your puppy home, the breeder should give you the puppy's identification papers. These include:

THE PEDIGREE: This chart of your Chihuahua's ancestry contains the sire's (father's) line on the top half of the pedigree, and the dam's (mother's) line along the bottom. Any dogs listed in the pedigree with a "Ch" in front of their names are champions. This tells you that they are outstanding examples of the breed standard.

Don't fall for the first cute puppy that you see. Instead, watch how puppies interact with each other and react to their surroundings. If you're a novice dog owner, you'll probably want a puppy that is neither too bold nor too timid.

Obedience, agility, and rally titles are listed after a dog's name. By looking at a dog's pedigree you can understand more about the physical conformation and accomplishments of your puppy's family.

REGISTRATION FORM: The breeder will fill out and sign the form to register your Chihuahua with the American Kennel Club (or another registry, such as the Canadian Kennel Club or the Kennel Club of the United Kingdom). You must sign the form as the dog's owner and submit it to the AKC, along with a registration fee. The American Kennel Club will send a completed registration certificate to you. Registration makes your Chihuahua eligible to compete in AKC-sponsored events

such as agility, obedience, and rally competitions.

Only dogs with full registration can participate in AKC conformation shows. Many reputable breeders will sell pet-quality puppies on an AKC limited registration. This means that they cannot be shown in AKC conformation events, and that any offspring they may produce will not be eligible for registration with the American Kennel Club.

SALES CONTRACT: This document is a bill of sale, but it includes health and quality guarantees and the terms of a refund or a replacement. Both you and the breeder will sign an agreement that you will care for this puppy and not resell him. Generally, if you buy a purebred puppy but at

RESEARCH YOUR PUPPY'S HEALTH

To learn more about your AKC-registered puppy's family health profile, check the Canine Health Information Center (CHIC) Web site, www.canine-healthinfo.org. This centralized health database maintained by the AKC/Canine Health Foundation and the Orthopedic Foundation for Animals (OFA) provides test results for breed-specific problems.

The Chihuahua Club of America recommends that breeders conduct health testing for patellar luxation, eye disease, and congenital heart disease. The results of these exams are posted on this site and updated when dogs are retested. The CHIC maintains a DNA bank and stores DNA samples for future research.

Studies have shown that pet owners typically live longer, are less stressed, and have fewer heart attacks than people who don't own pets. Studies have also shown that dogs handled and cared for in a loving manner are healthier overall.

some point find that you can no longer care for it, the breeder may have the option to take the dog back. She may also require you to have the Chihuahua puppy spayed or neutered by a certain age.

HEALTH RECORDS: The breeder should give you a copy of your puppy's health records, including his date of birth, visits to the veterinarian, and a list of all immunizations and parasite treatments. Bring these records with you when you take your Chihuahua to the veterinarian for his first checkup, which you should schedule within 48 hours of taking your Chihuahua home.

ADOPTING AN OLDER CHIHUAHUA

Chihuahua breed rescues, shelters, and breeders sometimes have healthy older puppies available for adoption. The Chihuahua Club of America and the Chihuahua breed club in your area may be able to refer you to breeders who want to place their older Chihuahuas with good families.

There are pros and cons to adopting an older Chihuahua. An adult Chihuahua is probably past the chewing stage, may already be housetrained, and might already have been taught to respond to some useful commands, such as "sit," "stay," and "come." Another advantage to adopting a mature Chihuahua is that medical surprises should be minimal. Health issues in older dogs are usually diagnosed and you'll know how to treat them rather than having to go through expensive medical testing to find out what's wrong. On the other hand, although many Chihuahuas available for adoption from shelters or breed rescue organizations are there through no fault of their own, some come with health or temperament issues. Some rescued Chihuahuas don't get along with other dogs, and some can't be placed with children, so if you have another dog or if there are children in your home, it may take longer to find an appropriate match.

In an effort to find the best homes for the dogs, Chihuahua rescue organizations ask potential new owners to fill out an adoption application. Rescue volunteers want to make sure adopted dogs remain in their new homes for the rest of their lives. Before you adopt a Chihuahua through a rescue organization, the dog should have a veterinary examination and be current on all vaccines. A female should be spayed, and a male neutered. The dog's temperament should also be evaluated.

Once you adopt a Chihuahua, it will take some time for your canine companion to adjust to your routine. If for any reason the Chihuahua doesn't work out, the rescue organization will accept the dog back.

Adoption is one of the most sensible, economical, and socially responsible methods of acquiring a new pet.

CHAPTER THREE

Bringing Home a Chihuahua

Whether you're purchasing a purebred puppy from a breeder or adopting an adult dog from a shelter, you'll probably have to wait a little while before you can take a new Chihuahua home. Use this time to prepare your household and family for the new arrival. Ask the breeder or rescue volunteer for a list of things your Chihuahua will need, and purchase these supplies before picking up your dog. Having everything on hand will help the transition from his kennel to your home go smoothly, and allows you to enjoy your Chihuahua's debut without having to leave for a shopping trip.

Don't forget dog food! Ask the breeder or rescue volunteer what

Shop for supplies before bringing your Chihuahua home for the first time.

kind of food your Chihuahua eats so you can have it on hand when he arrives. If your dog has been eating a packaged commercial dog food, it's best to keep feeding him the same brand for the first month or so. Over time, you can change to a different type of food if you want.

You'll need to dog-proof the house, too. Study your home's layout and locate any hazards that could be dangerous to your Chihuahua. This tiny breed can squeeze into very small spaces, and is likely to swallow tiny items that could cause internal injuries. Find a place in your home where your new pet can settle in and feel comfortable, and where he'll be safe from harm.

SHOPPING FOR ESSENTIALS

Things that your Chihuahua will need include a crate, dog bed, food and water bowls, a leash and collar, supplies for grooming and cleaning up after your dog, and fun toys.

The crate is an important item. You will use it to help train your Chihuahua, and it will help keep him out of trouble when you can't watch him. Crates can have hard plastic sides or collapsible wire frames. Choose a small crate: it should be just large enough for a full-grown Chihuahua to lie down while fully stretched out, and to easily stand up and turn around without hitting his head. An 18-inch or 22-inch (46 or 56 cm) crate works well for Chihuahuas.

Your Chihuahua should sleep in his crate at night, but you may also want to get a padded dog bed he can nap in during the daytime. These come in all shapes and sizes. Don't buy an expensive one until your dog is out of the chewing stage, which can last up to two years. If you're environmentally inclined, they even make surprisingly comfortable dog beds out of recycled soda bottles!

Don't purchase a larger crate thinking that you'll give your dog more room. You want to keep your Chihuahua in a relatively small space, because dogs generally will not potty where they sleep. If the crate is too large, he'll have room to go to the bathroom in the back of it, complicating your effort to house-train him.

Your dog will need a bowl for food and a separate bowl for water. While you'll find a wide assortment of glass, ceramic, plastic, and stainless steel options, choose bowls that can't tip over or slide across the floor. No-tip stainless steel bowls are easy to clean and will last forever. Avoid plastic bowls: although they are the cheapest, puppies love to chew on them and they're harder to keep clean and bacteria-free. To help keep the water cold, the water dish should be large and deep. The food dish only needs to hold about a half-cup of kibble.

Your dog will need a lightweight leather or web collar with a buckle. Avoid collars that snap closed, as this kind can slip right off a tiny Chihuahua's neck. The collar will carry your dog's identification tag, so that if he gets lost, the person who finds him can return him to you. Depending on the laws in your municipality, you may also have to attach tags showing that he's licensed and has had his rabies vaccination.

Make sure that these tags don't dangle too low, as they can get caught on something and choke your Chihuahua.

For outdoor exercise, your Chihuahua will need a leash. Choose a thin, four-foot leather or cotton-web leash, as this type seldom breaks and fits easily in your hand. The leash can be attached to the collar, although some Chihuahua owners prefer to attach it to a harness that goes around the dog's body.

Don't forget to purchase supplies to clean up after your Chihuahua. For housetraining accidents inside the house, purchase an enzyme-based stain and odor remover. If you don't fully remove the scent of urine using one of these products, your dog is likely to return and leave another mess in the same spot. For outside, purchase a pooper scooper or eco-friendly cleanup bags. Even though your small Chihuahua does-

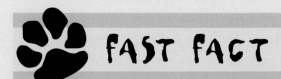

Most dogs love toys. They can provide exercise, mental stimulation, and comfort, especially if your Chihuahua spends a lot of time alone. Invest in sturdy chew toys, as Chihuahuas can destroy flimsy rubber toys fairly easily.

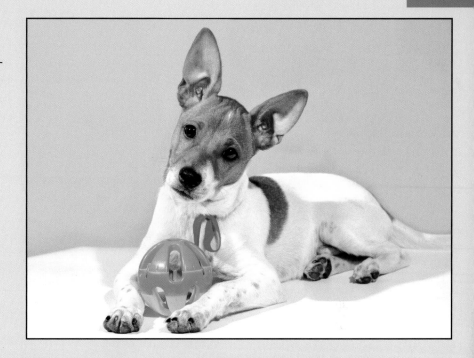

n't leave big messes in the yard, get in the habit of picking up his poop every day.

You'll also need grooming supplies (see Chapter 8) and some toys. When it comes to dog toys, you'll find a wide variety available. Avoid small balls and plush or squeaky toys that your dog can swallow or chew apart. Choose toys that are sturdy enough so your dog can't destroy them. Include one or two interactive items, or toys with places to tuck away treats, to keep your Chihuahua busy when he's left alone.

Some people like to dress up their Chihuahuas in fun or fancy outfits, but if you're on a budget don't bother buying dog clothes. Although dress-up clothes may look cute, they're expensive and unnecessary. The exception is that your Chihuahua will need a sweater to wear for walks or outdoor play in cold weather.

DOG-PROOFING YOUR HOME

When a Chihuahua moves into your home, his tiny size presents a unique set of challenges. He can accidentally get stepped on, fall off the couch or bed and become seriously injured, or catch a chill in a large, cold room. It's your responsibility to keep your pup safe in your home.

Before bringing a new pet into your home, lie on the floors in each room and look around. Seeing the

As soon as your Chihuahua puppy arrives at your home, he'll want to explore his new surroundings, both inside and out. Make sure that you've made the house and yard safe before letting him sniff around.

room from a puppy's perspective is the best way to discover hidden dangers. Remove hanging tablecloths and free-standing lamps, bundle loose electrical cords and pick up any small items on the floor, as these are all potential hazards.

Once you've done this, decide which rooms you will permit your Chihuahua to occupy. Put up baby gates or barriers to keep your dog out of rooms that either can't be made safe or contain valuable items you don't want him to chew.

In rooms where your dog will be allowed to roam, tack loose electrical cords to the wall or enclose them with cable wrap or a cord concealer. This will keep your dog from tripping over or chewing on them. Put all garbage in a bin with a tight-fitting lid, or store the wastebasket in a cabinet. In the bathroom put all hygiene products, used razor blades, medications, and cleaning supplies out of your dog's reach. Install child-proof locks on kitchen and bathroom cabinets so that your Chihuahua can't get into them.

When a Chihuahua lives in your house, you'll have to become a "neat freak." On a daily basis pick up any loose items, such as rubber bands, coins, paper clips, barrettes, and

metal twist ties. Children's toys are especially dangerous; many contain small pieces that your dog can chew and swallow. These can cause an intestinal blockage, requiring emergency surgery to remove. Leather items, particularly shoes, have a pleasant odor that dogs are drawn to, so keep these off the floor and away from tiny Chihuahua teeth.

There are plenty of dangers outside the house as well. In the yard, look along the bottoms of fences and gates for sharp edges that could hurt your dog, or for gaps through which he could escape. Make sure gates are secure. Fence off roses or other thorny plants that could injure eyes. Keep your Chihuahua away from poisonous plants, such as azaleas, holly bushes, and lilies. The American Society for the Prevention of Cruelty to Animals (ASPCA) has an extensive list of plants that are toxic to dogs on the Internet at

http://www.aspca.org/pet-care/poison-control/plants. Many houseplants are dangerous, so be sure to check inside your home and place them out of reach.

Garages and tool sheds usually contain antifreeze, paint thinner, gasoline, and other dangerous chemical substances. Antifreeze containing ethylene glycol is particularly dangerous. Its sweet flavor appeals to dogs, but ingesting even a teaspoon of it can be deadly. These areas also contain sharp tools and other items that can hurt your Chihuahua. It's best to make them off-limits for your dog.

COMING HOME

When the time finally comes to pick up your Chihuahua, choose a day that will enable you to spend one or more days at home with your new arrival. This will let your Chihuahua get to know you and allow him to

settle into his new home. Avoid bringing a new pet home before a major holiday, such as Thanksgiving or Christmas. Most households are noisy and hectic during these celebrations, and your Chihuahua could easily be neglected.

Your Chihuahua will need a quiet, stable environment to help him

Allow all members of your family to spend some time with your new puppy. Be careful not to overdo it, however, as a puppy can easily become overwhelmed. Remember that young children should never handle a puppy without adult supervision.

adjust to his new home. A puppy won't understand why he's been taken away from his mother and siblings and now lives in a strange place with unfamiliar people. The ride to your home will probably be his first time in a car. It will take some time for him to relax and feel comfortable, so don't rush the "getting acquainted" stage.

Adding a new dog to the family is an exciting event, but don't be in a hurry to show him off to everyone you know. When your Chihuahua arrives at his new home for the first time, give him a few minutes to sniff around in the rooms you have made safe for him. Show your Chihuahua where his food and water dishes will be kept. Then introduce him to all the members of your household, one person at a time. For the next two days or so, try to keep household activities low-key; this is not the time to start spring cleaning or hold a birthday party. Make you're your children don't smother your new Chihuahua with too much hugging, either, as this will only frighten him. Wait a week or so before inviting neighbors and extended family over so you don't overwhelm him.

Until his first day at your home, your puppy will have spent his entire life romping and sleeping alongside his mother and littermates. While he'll enjoy exploring his new surroundings and meeting your family, he'll also miss his brothers and sisters. Give him plenty of attention and play time the first few days. The distraction will help ease the transition to his new family.

THE FIRST NIGHT

On the first day your Chihuahua comes home, establish a schedule so that he'll know what to expect. This facilitates housetraining and helps the dog adapt to your routine. Feed him around the same times, and in the same place, each day. Try to keep to a regular schedule for playtimes and bedtime.

Puppies sleep a lot. Don't be alarmed if your Chihuahua pup suddenly plops down for a snooze in the middle of a game. Make sure he has plenty of rest time during the day—ideally, in his crate. This way he will become accustomed to his special place before it's time to go to bed at night. Although it may be tempting to let your puppy nap on your lap, don't make this a habit or he won't want to sleep on his own.

A good way to hopefully get your puppy to sleep through the first night in his crate is to put the crate next to your bed. Inside the crate, put a chew toy and a large stuffed animal, but first be sure to remove any plastic pieces he could swallow. The toy will give him something to do if he wakes up during the night, and the stuffed animal will be a comforting reminder of bunking with his littermates. About an hour before bedtime, play with your dog to tire him out, and take him outside to use the potty. When he's finished, put him in the crate and turn off the lights in your bedroom.

If he whimpers during the night, you can reassure him that you haven't abandoned him. When dogs are crated alone outside their owners' bedrooms, they're apt to bark and whimper the first few nights. If you think your dog has to use the potty, quickly take him outside. But don't talk to him or give him any extra attention because he'll think it's playtime. Return him to the crate and go back to sleep.

Resist the urge to let your Chihuahua sleep in your bed. He's so small that you could easily roll over and crush him in the night. He could easily fall or jump off the bed during the night, which could result in a serious injury.

CHAPTER FOUR

Responsible Chihuahua Ownership

Owning a Chihuahua comes with a great deal of responsibility. In addition to making sure that a pet is both healthy and happy, dog owners must meet basic requirements established by law. These include licensing dogs, ensuring that pets can be properly identified, and complying with noise ordinances and littering laws. A responsible owner knows and obeys all local laws related to dog ownership.

Dog owners must be considerate of neighbors and other members of the community. People will become annoyed if your Chihuahua barks incessantly or leaves messes on someone's lawn. As a dog owner, it is

Restraining your Chihuahua with a leash when in public will keep him safe and out of trouble.

your responsibility to make sure your dog is under control and to clean up after your dog.

LICENSING REQUIREMENTS

Every municipality within the United States requires pet owners to register and license their dogs. In most cases, this license must be renewed each year. Licenses can usually be purchased from the local courthouse or municipal office, or from your town's animal control officer. They may also be available from your veterinarians.

The cost of a license varies, depending on the municipality. In some places, you can get a discounted license if your dog has been spayed or neutered. Discounts may also apply if your dog has a perma-

nent form of identification, such as a tattoo or microchip.

Failure to get a license is considered a misdemeanor offense in many places. It typically results in a fine that is significantly higher than the cost of licensing your Chihuahua. Dog owners who want to avoid legal hassles should carefully follow the licensing requirements established for their community.

IDENTIFICATION

Dogs are generally required to wear collars and tags that identify their owners. Laws typically require that such tags include the owner's name and address; some may require a phone number as well. Dog owners should follow the rules of their municipality to avoid citations and fines.

On the Internet, you can find information about local laws and ordinances related to dog ownership.

Most communities require dogs to wear an ID tag in public, along with proof the dog has been registered with the animal control officer and has a current rabies vaccination.

your Chihuahua has some form of identification greatly increases his chances of being returned.

In addition to collar tags, there are two other common identification methods: tattooing and microchip implantation. Both methods are considered permanent techniques. Tattooing is the older of the two techniques, but it is no more reliable than microchip identification.

Tattooed dogs are marked with a series of numbers. In most cases, these numbers are the same as the owner's telephone number or the dog's AKC registration number. Common locations for the tattoo include the belly and the inside of the thigh. However, the tattoo can be placed on other sections of the body as well.

Tattooing can be a very effective identification method, but there are drawbacks to the procedure. Over time, the tattoo can fade so much that it becomes unreadable. Registering the tattoo can also be confusing. Multiple registries need to be contacted, and your contact information will have to be updated every time it changes.

Dog owners who are uncomfortable with tattooing can opt for microchip implantation instead. This high-tech method is similar to tattooing in that it attaches dogs to their

Even if you live in one of the few places where dogs don't need to wear tags, consider doing it anyway. According to the Humane Society, one in three pets will become lost at some point during their lifetimes, and only 20 percent of lost pets without collar ID will be reunited with their owners. Making sure that

own unique number. The difference is that the identification exists within a computer chip that is implanted under the dog's skin. The chip is about the size of a grain of rice and is delivered via a painless injection. Lost dogs that are turned in to a shelter can be scanned with a special hand-held microchip-reading device. The owner's contact information is stored in a pet-recovery database, so that the lost dog can be returned.

COMMON LEGAL ISSUES

Failure to properly license and provide ID for a dog isn't the only thing that can get a Chihuahua owner into trouble. Barking, trespassing, littering, and biting can also create legal problems.

Chihuahuas can be loud, annoying barkers, and it is up to their owners to keep barking under control. Many towns and cities have noise ordinances, which limit the loudness and the duration of sounds coming from residences and businesses. These regulations typically go into effect at night, when most people want to sleep. A dog that barks for an extended period at night is likely to violate the local noise ordinance. If neighbors complain to the police, that dog's owner may wind up paying a fine. Dogs that continue violating the local noise ordinance could be

taken away from their owners.

Allowing a Chihuahua to trespass on someone else's property is another recipe for trouble. If your dog destroys anything or makes a mess, you will be financially responsible for the damage. To avoid trouble, owners should be vigilant about keeping their dogs in their own yards. Cleaning up after any messes that a Chihuahua leaves behind is also important. The fines for not picking up a dog's waste in a public area can be considerable.

The most common legal problem dog owners face involves biting. According to the Centers for Disease Control and Prevention, dogs bite about 4.7 million people in the

Take precautions to make sure your Chihuahua doesn't bite someone.

United States every year. Medical treatment is required in more than 15 percent of these cases. Half of the people treated are children.

Chihuahua owners must minimize the chance that their dog will bite someone. Most dog bites happen on the owner's property, so posting a warning sign there is a good idea. Owners should also use a leash when walking their dogs. Extra precautions should be taken when a dog has displayed aggressive tendencies. In that case a responsible owner will find a way to control and correct the dog's behavior. This may require obedience training or the help of a behavioral specialist.

The consequences of biting can be severe. Dogs that cause serious injury may be put to death. The owners of dogs that bite are likely to face significant legal and financial penalties.

SPAYING OR NEUTERING

Spaying or neutering is another responsibility that must not be overlooked. These surgeries prevent unwanted pregnancies and help dogs live longer, healthier lives. Spaying a female Chihuahua can prevent uterine and ovarian cancer, and reduces the likelihood of breast cancer. Neutering a young male can eliminate the risk of testicular and prostate cancer.

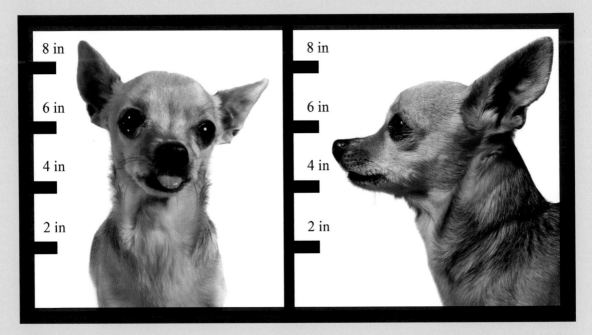

Your dog may find himself "wanted" by community groups or the local animal control officer if you allow him to misbehave by chasing cats or eliminating on a neighbor's property.

These procedures are also useful in eliminating or reducing certain problem behaviors common to the Chihuahua breed. Neutering reduces the likelihood that your male will roam, mark territory with urine, react aggressively to others, or attempt to mount a visitor's leg. Spaying females reduces the severity and incidence of their hormone-induced mood swings.

There are only two good reasons to refrain from spaying or neutering: breeding or showing. In the case of breeding, the explanation is obvious. In the case of showing, the explanation involves American Kennel Club rules. Conformation shows were originally developed to showcase breeding stock, so the AKC does not allow dogs that have been sterilized to participate in AKC-sanctioned conformation shows.

Chihuahuas can be spayed or neutered at six months of age. Both surgeries are relatively inexpensive and can be performed by any licensed veterinarian. Whenever possible, females should be spayed before their first heat cycle.

PET INSURANCE

Today, new treatments and medications make it possible for dogs to live a longer, healthier life. However, good veterinary care does not come cheap. According to the American Pet Products Association, dog owners in the United States spend more than $12 billion on veterinary care each year, with an additional $10 billion spent on pet supplies and over-the-counter-medications.

One option that could reduce the cost of your Chihuahua's health care is to purchase a pet insurance policy. Pet insurance reimburses policyholders for veterinary expenses, such as spaying/neutering and other surgeries, hospitalization, illnesses, accidents, and prescriptions. Some policies cover preventive care, such as annual checkups, teeth cleaning, parasite control, and health screenings.

Pet insurance policies can be purchased from various sources. Veterinarians don't normally sell policies, but they may be able to recommend a carrier. An Internet search can also turn up dozens of companies and organizations that provide health and life insurance plans for pets. Two of the best-known organizations are the American Society for the Prevention of Cruelty to Animals (ASPCA) and the American Kennel Club. Each offers nationally recognized insurance plans with varying levels of coverage.

The plans offered by the ASPCA, the AKC, and other pet insurance carriers are similar to health insurance plans for people. The dog owner pays an annual premium, the size of which depends on the insurance carrier, the level of coverage, the age of the dog, the geographic location, and other factors. Typically, pet insurance policies have a deductible, which means that the insurance carrier begins paying out claims only after the pet owner has spent a certain amount of money toward the dog's care. Most plans also include co-pays for each visit to the veterinarian.

To make sure that they are getting the best deal, Chihuahua owners should comparison-shop before buying an insurance policy. In addition to considering premiums, deductibles, and co-pays, dog owners are well advised to find out about exclusions and gaps in coverage. Every policy has some sort of exclusion. Most

involve preexisting conditions. You'll want to make sure that your policy covers conditions common among Chihuahuas, such as slipped kneecaps or molera-related damage.

Another factor worth investigating is the method by which the insurance carrier pays out claims. Some pay veterinarians directly, but most require the owner to pay up front and wait for reimbursement. Knowing which method is used before signing up for a policy is always a good idea.

A final consideration for Chihuahua owners is cost. Although a pet insurance plan can be a smart financial investment for some people, these policies do not pay off for everyone. In fact, it may cost more to pay the premiums, deductibles, and co-pays than it does to pay for veterinary care out of pocket.

CHAPTER FIVE

Raising a Better Chihuahua

It takes a lot of work to properly train and socialize a Chihuahua. The effort is worth it, though, because life with a well-behaved Chihuahua has many rewards. Chihuahuas are intelligent and willing to please, so all you'll need to succeed are positive training methods and plenty of practice.

For maximum effectiveness, use food tidbits, special toys, or affection as rewards for good behavior. When your dog knows that you are pleased with him, he will repeat the desired behavior. Praise him lavishly with an upbeat tone of voice when your dog does what you want. Avoid harsh methods like yelling, shaking, or hit-

Temperamentally, the ideal Chihuahua is confident and alert.

ting your dog, because studies have shown that these methods cause more harm than good.

Dogs thrive when they have a routine to follow. An erratic schedule of feeding, exercise, and potty times will confuse a young Chihuahua trying to learn the rhythm of his environment. To ease your dog's transition into your home, set up a structured schedule for him. For the first few weeks at least, keep a written chart of your dog's routine. Allot specific times for eating, sleeping, grooming, socialization, and training each day, and hang the schedule where everyone in your household can view it. Housetraining and obedience training will go smoothly when everyone understands your Chihuahua's needs.

If all family members stay consistent and follow the same rules, training a Chihuahua becomes much easier. Remember, training your dog should be a pleasant experience for everyone involved. Remain patient and enjoy the journey.

SOCIALIZATION

One of the most important things you can do for a Chihuahua puppy is to introduce him to new people, unfamiliar sights and sounds, and unknown dogs or other animals on a regular basis. This process, known as socialization, familiarizes your Chihuahua with the world around him.

Socializing a puppy is not a quick process. It takes time for a young Chihuahua to realize that people,

RESOURCE GUARDING

A young Chihuahua may act possessive about his food, toys, or sleeping area, growling and snapping when someone gets near his favorite things. This behavior, known as resource guarding, comes from his days of tussling with his littermates over such items. Nipping such behavior in the bud must be an integral part of your routine training. If your

Chihuahua attempts to guard his food, toy, or bed, don't ignore his bad manners. Instead, offer him a small food treat. When he accepts it, take the toy away or close his crate. If he's eating, take his food away and give it to him a half-hour later. It may take a few times, but eventually he'll realize that deferring to you is more important than guarding his treasured items.

other dogs, or strange objects won't hurt him. Socialization is particularly important during the first 16 weeks of a puppy's life, as it will help him to become a confident and friendly dog. A dog that is not properly socialized is more likely to be fearful, aggressive toward strangers, and harder to train.

Good socialization doesn't have to be a huge ordeal. In fact, a constant barrage of new experiences will only overwhelm your dog and erode, rather than boost, his confidence. Taking him outside your home for 10 to 20 minutes a day to visit one or two new places is plenty.

If you've purchased a purebred Chihuahua puppy from a reputable breeder, she will already have begun the socialization process. Continue with the process when you bring him home. Wearing his collar with ID tags and a leash, your dog can walk through a pet supply store, go for a walk around the neighborhood or outdoor mall, or ride in the car to visit friends. Meandering through a garden center, going to a park or playground, or observing a construction site that's shut down for the weekend will be fascinating for your Chihuahua. Wherever you decide to go, these outings should be short and fun.

When you encounter a friendly stranger, simply stop and chat. Your

Proper socialization involves introducing your Chihuahua to other friendly people and animals—even if they are as large as this Great Dane.

dog will sense your level of relaxation and enjoy the experience. If your Chihuahua seems hesitant around someone, ask the person if she wouldn't mind giving your dog a little treat. This creates a positive association with a stranger. Stay away from someone you don't feel comfortable meeting, because your pup will pick up on your discomfort. Let your pup observe adults and children, but don't let him jump on people.

When you encounter another dog when out for a walk, before stopping ask the owner whether her dog is gentle. Don't allow your Chihuahua

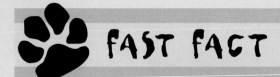

location has a pen for small dogs, such places can be very intimidating to a young Chihuahua. While he may meet other dogs his size, some may not be friendly, and once your dog is off his leash you'll have no control over his safety. Skip crowded places, also, as your Chihuahua could easily get stepped on while trying to dodge foot traffic and may feel intimidated by a large number of people.

Just because your dog is confident around the house, don't assume he doesn't need socialization. It's a different world outside your front door and your dog needs to safely explore. If you acquire your dog after four months of age, begin socializing him just as you would a puppy.

CRATE TRAINING

Think of a crate as your dog's personal luxury suite. With a comfy sleeping pad, a few toys, and just enough space to feel nice and cozy, this portable den serves many purposes. If your Chihuahua needs a respite from raucous children, larger pets, or the general hubbub of your household, the crate is a safe den where he can escape. It's also invaluable as a housetraining aid or as a safe way to transport your dog for a car ride. At the veterinarian's office your dog will be housed in a crate

to meet a new dog until you feel comfortable with the situation. Watch both of them, and don't let your dog become too exuberant or get too close to the other dog. You can't guarantee another dog's behavior.

If something frightens your Chihuahua, don't coddle him or make a fuss. This will only reinforce his insecurity. Instead, ignore his fear and act as though there's nothing wrong. Your dog will pick up on your confident attitude.

Avoid taking your Chihuahua to socialize in a dog park. Even if this

following any surgical procedures, so the sooner you train your dog to feel comfortable in a crate, the better.

Your dog needs time to adjust to his place. Introduce it gradually over several days. For the first session, set up the crate and place a few toys and a blanket inside. Let your dog sniff it out. Encourage him to explore the interior by tossing a treat into the back of the crate. If he wanders in, praise him and quietly close the door for a few seconds. Then praise him again, open the door, and give him

another treat when he comes out. Repeat this several times, gradually extending the time your dog is inside the crate to about 10 minutes. Then put him in the crate again, but this time leave the room for one minute before returning to let him out. Gradually lengthen the time you're gone to 30 minutes.

If your dog simply stands in front of the crate and looks in, encourage him to go after the goodies with some upbeat words. Come dinnertime, put his feeding dish inside the

VISITING DOG PARKS

Taking dogs to fenced-in dog parks is becoming more popular. Unfortunately, these play areas aren't always the best option for a Chihuahua. Other dogs can play too rough, and many owners don't supervise their dogs as closely as they should. An insecure Chihuahua can feel intimidated, and probably won't enjoy other dogs pouncing and chasing them. On the other hand, an aggressive Chihuahua may not know how to play nicely with other dogs.

If you go to a dog park, make sure the yard is divided into separate areas for small and large dogs. Observe the level of play before entering, as collisions with other dogs can injure your Chihuahua.

Examine the fencing to make sure that there are no openings through which your dog can escape if he becomes frightened. Once your Chihuahua is inside the dog park, keep an eye on his body language to judge how he may be feeling. If you sense a fight coming on, don't hesitate to remove your dog as quickly as possible.

crate to encourage him to go inside. This usually does the trick. When you decide to put your Chihuahua in his crate for the evening, place the crate next to your bed. This way you can talk to him and reassure him that you haven't abandoned him. Don't put the crate in another room away from you, as this can be scary to your dog and he'll surely make a fuss.

Keep a can of treats near the crate. Whenever you want him to go inside, shake the container and call your dog at the same time. When he comes to you, throw a treat from the can into the crate. He'll associate the treat with the pleasant experience of going to his bed.

HOUSETRAINING

Some owners say that Chihuahuas, and Toy breeds in general, are difficult to housetrain. They claim it's because the dogs aren't smart, have tiny or weak bladders, or are too stubborn to be properly house-

Encouraging your Chihuahua to do his business in the same spot outside the house, and rewarding him when he does this, can help facilitate housetraining.

trained. Don't believe these excuses. The truth is that Chihuahuas are intelligent, fully capable of controlling their bodily functions, and really want to please their owners. Housetraining problems start when a dog isn't reliably trained at an early age and begins developing bad habits. Some owners stall the housetraining process because it does require time and patience, and because a Chihuahua puppy's accidents are so small. When these owners do spot messes, they feel it's easier to clean them up rather than follow proper training techniques.

One issue that can complicate potty training is that most Chihuahuas don't like getting their feet wet. If you let your dog out when it's cold and rainy, he will try to hold his bladder and bowels as long as possible. Inexperienced owners may think that their dog doesn't need to go potty if he doesn't go right away, and may bring him back inside too soon. Next thing they know, there's an accident on the carpet.

Communicating that the carpets and floors of your house are not bathrooms can be a daunting task for a novice dog owner. It doesn't have to be hard. Begin taking your Chihuahua outside as soon as you bring him home. Designate a place in the yard where you'd like your dog to eliminate. A ten-week-old puppy is not too young to learn where the bathroom is. Develop a regular routine: take your puppy outside as soon as he wakes up in the morning, after every meal, following his naps, and every 20 to 30 minutes during the hours that he's awake. Puppies need to eliminate more frequently than adult dogs.

Chihuahuas like to keep themselves clean and won't mess where they sleep, so watch your dog carefully whenever he's out of the crate. It helps to restrict the area in which you allow your puppy to roam. Choose one or two rooms where you spend most of your time, and close the doors or place baby gates across all other doorways. This way you can keep an eye out for when your dog needs to go outside without having to search the whole house to find him. If you can't

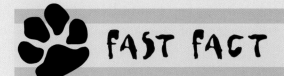

FAST FACT

Always keep a collar or harness and a leash on your Chihuahua whenever you take your dog outdoors. Chihuahuas can quickly dart away if they become frightened or decide to run after another dog, which puts them at risk for getting hit by a car or attacked by a larger dog.

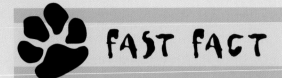

FAST FACT

A puppy kindergarten class can be a great aid to training and socializing your Chihuahua. Puppy kindergarten classes are designed for dogs between two to five months of age. They help new owners and their pups learning in a structured, low-key, and positive environment. Regular sessions give puppies an opportunity to interact with other puppies and build their confidence. Typical classes permit off-leash play and teach dogs how to remain gentle around other pups. Your puppy will also be introduced to other people and objects, and will learn how to relax in new settings and situations.

monitor his behavior for short periods, put him inside the crate. Watch your dog's body language. Signs that a Chihuahua needs to go outside include squatting, turning in circles or pacing back and forth, and sniffing the ground intently. If you see any of these signs, quickly pick your dog up and carry him outside.

Any time you retrieve your puppy from his crate, immediately take him to the potty area and say, "go potty!" When your dog does his business in the right place, reward him with kind words and praise. Make a fuss over him so there's no question that

you're happy with his behavior. Repeat the "go potty" command, or a similar cue phrase like "do your business," every time you take your dog out to eliminate.

If your Chihuahua has an accident inside the house, never yell, hit, or rub your dog's nose in the mess. This is cruel and doesn't work. Your dog will simply try to hide from you the next time he has to eliminate, and will leave messes where you can't immediately find them. If you see your dog going potty inside, wipe the pee or pick up the poop in a paper towel, then pick him up and take him to the designated outdoor potty place. Wipe the towel or drop the poop in the potty place, then praise your dog as though he had gone to the bathroom there intentionally. He'll get the idea. Make sure to clean up household messes with an enzymatic cleaner. These products contain proteins that break down stains and dissolve odors. This discourages your dog from returning to the same spot to urinate or defecate.

TEACHING BASIC MANNERS

All dogs must be taught the basic manners required for living with humans. The best time to establish household rules is when you first get a puppy. The rules are up to you, but generally they will include not begging for food at the dining table, not jumping on family members or guests to greet them, not barking incessantly, and not jumping on the furniture.

Don't allow your Chihuahua puppy to do things you would not find acceptable in an adult dog. If, for example, you allow your pup on furniture, he will want to lounge there as an adult. If you are sure that will be okay with you, go ahead and invite him onto the couch. However, if you don't want an adult Chihuahua on your sofa or bed, set that rule while your pup is young and stick to it.

If you start with one set of rules,

GETTING HELP WITH TRAINING

With time, patience, and positive reinforcement you can train a Chihuahua to do practically anything. Begin by socializing your dog and enrolling him in a puppy kindergarten class. An older Chihuahua can join an obedience class or you can hire a private trainer.

Choose a class or private trainer wisely. Ask the instructor about her qualifications. While anyone can say they are a dog trainer, look for a trainer with experience who is a member of a professional training organization, such as the Association of Pet Dog Trainers (www.apdt.com), the International Association of Animal Behavior Consultants (www.iaabc.org), or the National Association of Dog Obedience Instructors (www.nadoi.org). This indicates that the person is serious about training dogs and has met professional dog training requirements.

Observe a class before signing up. This gives you an opportunity to see the teacher's training style and watch her students with their dogs. A trainer should use reward-based training, which gives your dog the opportunity to work for bonuses, such as food, playtime, or affection that motivates him to perform desirable behavior. Avoid any trainer who uses punitive methods like hitting or shaking that can harm your dog. A good instructor should explain and demonstrate her training methods. A class should be small enough to provide individual attention. If there are more than six to eight student dogs, the trainer should have an assistant.

Look for a trainer who has experience with small dogs and who keeps up-to-date with new training methods. If your Chihuahua has a problem behavior, such as barking or aggressive behavior, the trainer should feel comfortable working with you and your dog.

Consistency is the key to successful training. If you don't think you'll want your Chihuahua climbing onto your sofas or chairs when he's an adult, don't allow him to sit on the furniture when he's a puppy.

then try to change them when your dog gets older, he'll become confused. It's much harder to change an established habit than install a good one, so think about how you'll want your Chihuahua to behave as an adult, then help him learn those behaviors while he's young and impressionable.

Consistency is one of the hall-

marks of good training technique. Make sure you give your Chihuahua consistent guidelines to follow, and enforce the rules you set up fairly. If your dog doesn't follow your instructions, don't make excuses for him just because of his size. Somehow, cute little Chihuahua puppies have a way of charming their owners into forgiving their errant behavior.

BASIC OBEDIENCE TRAINING

Your Chihuahua puppy can begin learning basic obedience commands, such as "sit," "stay," "down," and "come," a few days after you bring him home. Set aside five to ten minutes a day for this training. Make your sessions a regular part of your daily routine and keep them positive and fun experiences. Your dog will respond faster when lessons are enjoyable.

Your body language can help or hinder the training process. Avoid towering over your dog, waving your arms wildly, making sudden fast movements, or speaking in a harsh voice. These behaviors can intimidate a little dog. If your Chihuahua is frightened, he won't be motivated to focus on you. Instead, try sitting on the floor when teaching your Chihuahua and use a cheery, upbeat tone when talking to him. He'll pay closer attention and will be more likely to do what you want.

When you use treats as a training reward, remember to cut them in small pieces so he can gobble them quickly and easily. You don't want your dog spending precious training time chewing and swallowing when you need him to focus on the next lesson. Before beginning basic instructions for "sit," "stay," "down," and "come," teach him to pay attention to you. Call his name. As soon as he looks at you, give him a tiny food treat and say, "good boy." Repeat several times throughout the day.

To teach the "sit" command, hold a treat up over your dog's nose and

Prong or choke chains and shock collars should never be used on a Chihuahua. They can cause serious damage to your dog's trachea.

slowly move it back over his head as you say, "sit." As he moves his head to follow the treat with his eyes, he will naturally drop into a sitting position. When he does, immediately give him the treat and tell him he's a good dog. With a few repetitions, your dog will understand and obey the "sit" command.

Once your dog knows how to sit, teach him the "stay" command. After telling him to sit, say, "stay." Take a few steps backward. If he remains in the stay position for a few seconds, praise him and say, "OK." Then move toward him so he knows he can get up, and give him a treat. Repeat this several times. Gradually back up a few more steps each time, until you are about 10 feet away from your dog, and gradually extend the time you require your dog to maintain the "stay" position.

To teach the "down" command, start with your dog in a sitting position. Hold a treat in front of him and slowly lower it. This will naturally draw your Chihuahua downward until he is stretched out and lying down. When he reaches that position, immediately give him the treat and praise him. Repeat the exercise until he understands what you want when you say, "down."

The "come" command can be a lifesaver. You may need to use this command if your dog bolts into oncoming traffic or decides to wander away. To teach the command, fill a coffee can with biscuits. While inside the house, shake the can and say your dog's name followed by "come." When he comes to you, lavishly praise him and give him a treat. Once he responds reliably indoors, move to a fenced-in outdoor area to practice the command. Your dog

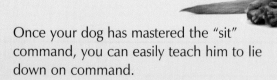

Once your dog has mastered the "sit" command, you can easily teach him to lie down on command.

Using a clicker and a food treat to reinforce your dog's positive behavior has become a popular training method. A clicker is a hand-held small plastic box that makes a loud clicking sound when you squeeze it.

should never be allowed off-leash in an open or public area until he has learned to respond to the "come" command every time.

Taking your dog for a walk should be a pleasure and not a chore. Without training, however, your Chihuahua is likely to pull at his leash. To teach him not to pull, simply stop walking when the leash goes taut. Don't begin walking again until the lease is loose. Eventually your dog will realize that trying to drag you around will get him nowhere.

CHAPTER SIX

Feeding 101

Small dogs have high metabolisms and require a lot of calories to keep going, but their small stomach capacity limits the amount of food these breeds can eat. Therefore, every bite your Chihuahua consumes must provide maximum nutrition to keep him in good health. This can be a challenge, as individual Chihuahuas can have very different eating habits. Some Chihuahuas are hearty eaters, while others pick at their food. To maintain your Chihuahua's health, it is very important to feed him nutritionally balanced, high-quality meals.

When deciding what to feed your dog, consider the quality of the

Your Chihuahua will be interested in whatever you're eating, but don't feed him scraps from the table. Doing this even once will simply encourage your dog to beg for food in the future. Never feed your dog cooked bones, as they can splinter and puncture your dog's intestines.

ingredients, the amount of energy it provides, and whether your dog likes the food and will eat it. Feeding your dog the best diet you can afford has many benefits. Good nutrition provides the structural components, vitamins, and minerals necessary for building and strong muscles and bones. A complete and balanced meal plan improves a dog's immune system, maintains coat and skin health, and promotes a longer life.

READ THE LABEL

How can you know whether your dog food offers enough nutrition? If you're buying a commercial food, look at the label printed on the package or can. The Association of American Feed Control Officials (AAFCO) provides an analysis of the ingredients, calories, and nutritional adequacy of the food. While this does not guarantee the food's quality, it means that the food is nutritionally balanced and complete according to

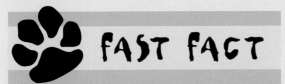

FAST FACT

Dry kibble is economical, and it provides the added benefit of helping to clean your Chihuahua's teeth. As he chews, the hard kibble will scrape plaque and tartar off the tooth enamel.

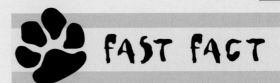

FAST FACT

When changing your dog's diet, do it gradually over seven to ten days. Mix in a little of the new food with the old, slowly increasing the ratio.

AAFCO guidelines. The AAFCO requires dry adult food to contain a minimum of 18 percent protein and 5 percent fat. Puppy food must have at least 22 percent protein and 8 percent fat.

The order in which the ingredients are listed on the AAFCO label reflects their proportions in the food, from highest percentage to lowest. The first ingredient listed should be an animal protein, such as beef, poultry, or lamb. Another protein source should be listed second or third. Avoid foods that include "meat by-products" among the first three ingredients. These by-products consist of animal parts that are not fit for human consumption, such as beaks, feat, feathers, and horns. They can also include meat from roadkill or from euthanized dogs.

The ingredients list should also contain carbohydrates, fats, vitamins and minerals, preservatives, and fiber. Carbohydrates and fats provide energy, while the combination of minerals, vitamins, and fiber all contribute to peak functioning. The nutritional adequacy statement on the label tells whether the food is designed for puppies, adults, seniors, or growth. While the AAFCO establishes feeding trial guidelines, the label doesn't ensure that the food has been tested to determine how a dog thrives on the diet.

COMMERCIAL FOODS

Kibble, or dry food, is the most popular way to feed dogs. It's convenient, economical, and tends to be low in fat, which will help keep your

FOOD ADDITIVES TO AVOID

When comparing brands of commercial dog food, be on the lookout for artificial ingredients. Inferior dog foods contain nine ingredients that you should avoid:

1. Butylated hydroxyanisole (BHA) or butylated hydroxytoluene (BHT). These preservatives prevent spoilage and extend shelf life. However, some studies indicate that they may cause cancer. Better recipes use vitamin C and vitamin E (mixed tocopherols) as preservatives. Unfortunately, foods with these preservatives don't last as long as foods with BHA or BHT.

2. Ethoxyquin. This preservative is linked to impaired liver and kidney function.

3. Propylene glycol. This liquid is used to prevent the food from drying out, but it may cause central nervous system impairment and changes in kidney function.

4. Phosphoric acid. A clear liquid, phosphoric acid serves as a flavoring agent and an emulsifier that prevents discoloration. It may irritate skin and mucous membranes.

5. Propyl gallate. A powerful antioxidant that prevents fats and oils from spoiling, propyl gallate is known to cause an allergic reaction in some dogs and has been linked to cancer.

6. Coloring agents. Red dye 40 and yellow dye 5 brighten food, but they have been linked to cancer.

7. Sorbitol. A synthetic sugar substitute used to flavor food, Sorbitol may cause diarrhea and intestinal upset, especially in large quantities.

8. DI-alpha tocopheryl acetate. This synthetic form of vitamin E is not easily absorbed.

9. Menadione sodium bisulfate vitamin K3. This synthetic form of vitamin K may irritate mucous membranes.

Chihuahua's weight in check. Unfortunately, not all dry foods are created equal. Many brands of kibble are labeled nutritionally complete because they contain the required minimum amounts of nutrients. Still, some brands contain the highest-quality ingredients while others do not. Look for a commercial dry food that contains whole meat (chicken, turkey, beef, lamb, or fish), and avoid foods with animal by-products. Carbohydrate sources in high-quality kibble often include vegetables like sweet potatoes or grains like barley or quinoa. These cause fewer allergies than corn, rice and wheat, which are commonly found in low-grade dry food.

While some Chihuahuas gobble down everything you give them, others may turn up their noses at dry food. Some owners will add a little warm water or a few spoonfuls of low-sodium chicken broth to the kib-ble, enticing their dogs to finish their meals. Others will add a tablespoon of canned food, or some fresh steamed or finely diced fruits or vegetables.

Many Chihuahua owners like feeding their dogs canned food because its strong aroma and flavor is appealing. Generally, though, they will use canned food to make dry kibble more palatable. It's not a good idea to feed your dog canned food exclusively, for several reasons. Canned food is more expensive than dry food because it contains a higher ratio of meat to grain. Canned food also contains a much higher percentage of water, so a dog must eat more of this type of food in order to obtain adequate nutrition. This can

Dog food does not have to be inspected before it is sold and sometimes it becomes contaminated, prompting the manufacturer to announce a recall. To determine if your Chihuahua's food has been recalled, check the ASPCA Web site, www.aspca.org.

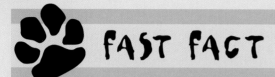

lead to obesity. In addition, canned food tends to stick to a dog's teeth and can be a source of dental disease. Kibble, on the other hand, helps to scrape plaque and tartar off a dog's teeth, keeping them cleaner.

After opening a can of food and doling out your Chihuahua's portion, cover and store what's left in the refrigerator. It will remain fresh for two days. If your dog leaves food in his bowl, give him 20 minutes to finish it. After that, discard it before the food spoils.

For owners who would like to feed their dogs a raw diet, but don't have the time to prepare it properly, frozen and dehydrated foods have become a popular alternative. These organic foods use human-grade ingredients and are prepared with minimal processing. They are nutritious and easy to feed: just defrost a frozen portion, or add a little warm water to a dehydrated meal, and supplement with a small serving of fresh fruits and vegetables. Uneaten portions can be refrigerated for up to two days. You can purchase these foods from pet supply stores or by mail order, but the cost is likely going to be higher than canned or dry foods.

HOME-COOKED MEALS

A growing number of dog owners are deciding to feed their dogs home-cooked meals. This does not simply involve giving your Chihuahua a plate of leftovers, however. Home-cooked meals must contain well-balanced nutrition in the proper proportion of ingredients to ensure maximum health.

There are advantages and disadvantages to making your dog's food. The biggest drawback is the time required. The biggest benefit is knowing exactly what your dog is eating. You can choose the ingredients according to your Chihuahua's needs. If you want to improve the quality of your dog's coat, for

example, you can increase the fat content slightly.

Before starting to feed your Chihuahua a home-cooked diet, discuss it with your veterinarian. In a typical diet, a source of protein such as cooked lean chicken, turkey, duck, beef, lamb, venison, pork, or fish should make up 30 to 60 percent of the meal. Carbohydrates in the form of cooked grains, such as brown rice, millet, barley, potatoes, rolled oats, or winter squash, should make up another 30 to 60 percent. Vegetables or fruit can make up 10 to 30 percent of the meal. Raw fruit is OK if it is finely chopped. Lightly steam green beans, broccoli, summer squash, cauliflower, carrots, and spinach. Include a calcium and phosphorus supplement, and add one or two teaspoons of salmon oil to provide omega-3 fatty acids. Your dog should also eat a regular canine multivitamin/mineral supplement, but check with your veterinarian for the proper dosage.

RAW DIETS

A raw diet is meant to resemble what a dog would eat in the wild. This type of diet excludes not only all commercial dog foods but also all cooked foods. Some dog owners believe that cooking food at high temperatures destroys vitamins, enzymes, and antioxidants. Raw diets are often used with dogs that have medical issues such as allergies or arthritis,

If you're concerned about your Chihuahua's nutrition, speak with your veterinarian. She should be able to recommend how much food your dog should eat, suggest a proper feeding schedule, and even identify the type of food that would be appropriate

when no other remedies seem to work. Other benefits that proponents tout include less doggy odor, naturally clean teeth, less stool production, better overall health, and less expense than a commercial food diet.

One well-known example is the Biologically Appropriate Raw Foods (BARF) diet, created by Dr. Ian Billinghurst. It includes raw bones and meat, some vegetables, and a few carbohydrates. Raw chicken bones, carcasses, wings, and necks are typically used. If raw meaty lamb, beef, venison, duck, rabbit, pig, or whole fish is more readily available, however, owners can use these sources.

Diets containing raw chicken or meat do have a few risks. Uncooked chicken or meat can harbor salmonella and E. coli bacteria. While salmonella is mild in dogs, infected dogs can carry the bacteria in the saliva and feces. Using organic-certified raw meat raised without antibiotics or hormones is the safest option, and it's best to purchase raw ingredients at their freshest and keep them refrigerated. Make sure that raw meaty bones are large enough that your dog can't swallow them.

FEEDING BASICS

Whether you choose to feed your Chihuahua a homemade diet or buy a commercial dog food, serve his meal in small, bite-size pieces. Tiny dogs have tiny mouths, and you don't want your Chihuahua to choke

If your dog is a picky eater, don't fill him up with treats during the day. Offer treats sparingly; otherwise your dog won't eat his regular food at all. When you do give your dog a treat, it should contain the same quality ingredients as his regular food. Treats should never consist of more than about 10 percent of your dog's daily caloric intake.

on a large piece of meat or break a tooth.

If you wonder whether the recipe you're giving your dog agrees or disagrees with him, look at his skin and coat and watch what he does. A healthy coat should always look glossy without any signs of dandruff. He should not develop skin irritations, so if your Chihuahua licks or chews at his feet obsessively or scratches constantly, he may be eating something that's not appropriate. Your dog should also not have frequent bouts of diarrhea or vomiting, and should not be excessively gassy.

Avoid diets containing mostly wheat, corn, soy, gluten, and by-products, as these ingredients are often the causes of dietary allergies.

When you bring a Chihuahua puppy home at around twelve weeks of age, he'll need to eat three or four meals a day. By the time he's four to six months old, you can gradually eliminate one meal, until you're feeding him twice a day. Adult Chihuahuas should have two meals a day.

Some people leave food out all day, especially if their dog is a little fussy and doesn't finish it all at one

AVOID LOW BLOOD SUGAR

Hypoglycemia, or low blood sugar, is a life-threatening condition in many toy breeds. It is relatively common among Chihuahua puppies under 12 weeks old. When glucose levels in the blood drop rapidly, the body and brain are deprived of nutrients and the dog may become weak and suffer seizures.

A Chihuahua that suddenly starts wobbling when he walks, or falls down, may be suffering from low blood sugar. Other warning signs include a dog that seems unusually sleepy or lethargic. Although the condition is triggered by a lack of nutrition, the dog may refuse to eat.

For a quick remedy, rub some Karo syrup or honey on your dog's gums or on the roof of his mouth. You can also give him a little Nutrical, a malt-flavored paste with sugar and vitamins, which is available at a pet supply store. His gums will quickly absorb the sugar, raising his blood sugar until you can get your puppy to the veterinarian.

To avoid hypoglycemia, feed your dog several small meals a day. Some people believe that fresh foods, rather than a commercial diet, help maintain a consistent glucose levels.

time. This practice, known as "free feeding," isn't recommended. First of all, dogs that dine at their leisure usually become overweight. Second, you'll have difficulty monitoring how much your dog is actually eating. This can be a problem because loss of appetite may signal an illness that requires the veterinarian's attention.

It's best to feed your dog on a regular schedule—breakfast and dinner. Use a measuring cup so you can regulate the portion size. Your Chihuahua will probably eat 1/4 to 1/2 cup of food at each meal. Start by offering him a half-cup of food at meals; if he gobbles that down and hangs around the kitchen looking for more, increase the amount slightly. If he tends not to eat that much, after a few meals you can reduce the amount of food he is served. Typically, a puppy will eat more than a senior Chihuahua that has a lower activity level.

Obesity is a major health problem for dogs, and can lead to diabetes, bone and joint diseases, heart and lung diseases, urinary disorders, skin conditions, and some types of cancer. Simply put, extra body weight shortens a dog's life expectancy. The best way to tell whether your dog is getting too much food is by rubbing the skin on his sides. If you can't feel the ribs, he's carrying too much weight.

CHAPTER SEVEN

Keeping Your Chihuahua Healthy

Well-bred, properly cared for Chihuahuas can live long, healthy lives. Twelve to 15 years is the average lifespan, although some Chihuahuas can make it to their 20th birthdays. To keep your dog in prime condition, feed him a healthy diet, provide daily exercise, and visit the veterinarian at least once a year for a wellness checkup.

If you're looking for a veterinarian, ask for referrals from your breeder, rescue coordinator, or friends with dogs. You might also want to contact the American Animal Hospital Association (www.healthy-pet.com) for a list of recommended

Annual checkups by the veterinarian are essential for your Chihuahua's quality of life.

veterinarians in your area.

When selecting a vet, consider emergency arrangements, facilities, and services. Find out whether the vet attends veterinary conferences to learn about new techniques. Before making a decision, it's a good idea to tour facilities and make an appointment to speak with the vet personally. Ask what kind of experience the veterinarian has with Toy breed dogs, and Chihuahuas in particular. The vet's answers to your questions should be clear and you shouldn't feel rushed, but expect to pay for the veterinarian's time.

Take your new Chihuahua to the veterinarian for her first checkup a day or two after you bring her home. Assuming your dog is healthy, the visit should be a positive experience and a chance for your doctor to learn about your dog. Bring a fresh stool sample with you so the vet can check for intestinal parasites. During the routine visit the veterinarian should weigh your dog, listen to her heart and lungs, take her temperature, check her pulse, and examine her coat, skin, eyes, ears, feet, and mouth.

Discuss an overall health care plan for your Chihuahua, including flea, tick, and heartworm preventives, as well as a vaccine schedule. Find out about spaying if your dog is a female, or neutering if your dog is a male. You might also want to review your dog's diet.

VACCINATIONS AND TITERS

To prevent certain diseases, veterinarians once vaccinated dogs every year. Today the protocol is different. Studies have shown that administering too many canine vaccinations can compromise a dog's immune system. The American Animal Hospital Association recently issued a new set of vaccination guidelines, recommending that vaccines should be administered once every three years.

Puppies need an initial series of core vaccines to protect them from canine diseases. These include distemper, adenovirus, and parvovirus core vaccines at 9 to 10 weeks, 14 weeks, and 16 to 18 weeks, with a booster given at one year. Following this series, the distemper, adenovirus, and parvovirus core vaccines

should be administered once every three years.

The one vaccine required by law is the rabies vaccine. You must show proof of rabies vaccination to get a dog license, board her in a kennel, or take her on an airplane. The first rabies vaccine should be given at 20 weeks or older. The frequency of required booster shots for rabies varies by state and municipality.

Noncore vaccinations for coronavirus, canine parainfluenza virus, leptospirosis, Lyme disease, and kennel cough (bordetella) should be given when the risk of the disease is significant. Your veterinarian will be able to advise you.

After the initial core vaccines, your veterinarian can measure the levels of protective antibodies already present in the system, called titers, by drawing a blood sample. A high titer count reveals a high level of immunity to the disease, while a low titer count indicates that a dog is still susceptible. Many veterinarians recommend using these titer tests before vaccinating a dog again. Titers are not available for bordetella, parainfluenza, or coronavirus.

Some Chihuahuas have shown an adverse reaction to leptospirosis vaccine, or to the preservatives and adjuvants in vaccines that enhance the immune response. Symptoms of

COCCIDIA AND GIARDIA

Coccidia is a common protozoal infection that can infect puppies raised in overcrowded, unsanitary kennels. It takes 13 days from the time a puppy is exposed to coccidia before he becomes ill. Symptoms include mild to severe cases of intermittent watery or bloody diarrhea. Serious cases can be fatal. The veterinarian can detect the problem by examining a dog's stool sample under the microscope. Drugs take one to three weeks to prevent the organisms from reproducing, but cannot kill them. Cleaning up feces and providing clean water helps prevent coccidia.

Bloody diarrhea and vomiting may be a sign of giardia, a microscopic organism that lives in contaminated outdoor sources of water. This organism attacks a dog's intestinal tract. If a dog laps up contaminated water from a stream or puddle he may become infected. Medication is available to treat severe cases.

mild vaccine sensitivity can include fever, lethargy, poor appetite, and temporary pain and muscle soreness. In more serious cases, vomiting, diarrhea, respiratory distress, or physical swelling can occur. If you notice any symptoms after vaccines are given, report them immediately to your veterinarian and seek emergency treatment.

EXTERNAL PARASITES

Fleas, ticks, and mites are nasty pests that can drive a dog crazy—and can compromise your dog's health. Chihuahuas are too small to spare blood for these parasites. The effects of a flea infestation range from skin irritation to severe allergic reactions. Fleas also transmit tapeworms to dogs. To get rid of fleas, treat your dog, her bedding, the entire inside of your house, and the yard. Contact your veterinarian to obtain a spot-on flea treatment and an oral insect-growth regulator treatment. Be diligent about using them every month.

Ticks are potentially very danger-ous. They transmit Lyme disease, Rocky Mountain spotted fever, ehrlichiosis, and tick paralysis. Ticks cling to bushes and inhabit wooded areas. They can leap onto a dog's head, back, or neck when she passes by. To prevent ticks, keep the grass short around your home, and remove tall bushes. If you take your Chihuahua walking through wooded or mountainous areas, spray him with a product that kills ticks.

After outdoor outings, check your Chihuahua for ticks. They can be found anywhere, although they seem particularly fond of clinging to ears, the tail area, or even between the toes. If you see a tick on your dog, remove it immediately. Use tweezers to gently grasp near the head and pull the tick off. Flush the tick down the toilet. Apply a little hydrogen peroxide to your dog at the site of the tick attachment or bite.

Microscopic ear mites can cause otodectic mange, a condition that affects the outer ear canal by causing persistent infections. These mites burrow into the lining of a Chihuahua's ear canals, triggering intense itching, scratching, redness, and a foul odor. If you notice your dog shaking and tilting his head or rubbing his ears on the carpet, suspect ear mites. Dogs pick up these mites from other dogs. The veterinarian can detect them by examining the ears with an otoscope. Treatment includes flushing out the ear canal, applying medication, and massaging the ear once a day. A full month of treatment is required to eliminate these pesky mites.

HEARTWORM

Transmitted by mosquitoes, heartworms are internal parasites that can be deadly to dogs if left untreated. The larvae of these parasites circulate through the dog's bloodstream. In the adult stage, heartworms travel to the right side of the heart. Reaching lengths of up to 12 inches, they can totally engulf that organ.

Once prevalent in the United States only in the South, heartworms are now found in most areas of the country. Your veterinarian can prescribe a preventive medication for you to give your dog once a month.

Heartworm medication can also be used to prevent other internal parasites such as hookworms, roundworms, and whipworms. Roundworms are common in puppies and can easily be killed with medication. Whipworms are more difficult to destroy.

CHIHUAHUA ILLNESSES

Like every breed, Chihuahuas are prone to general illnesses as well as certain genetic conditions. To have the best chance of getting a healthy canine companion, buy your Chihuahua from a reputable breeder who belongs to the Chihuahua Club of America. Before breeding two dogs, CCA breeders test the mother and father for certain inherited conditions, such as breathing problems, heart murmurs, liver shunts, and patellar luxation (slipped kneecaps). When dogs are tested, they are identified by a microchip and a DNA profile. Results are recorded with the Canine Health Information Center (CHIC) database.

Even with this testing, there is no guarantee your puppy will grow into a perfectly healthy dog that will live to a ripe old age. However, parents free from genetic health issues are less likely to produce offspring that will develop an inherited disease. Also, reputable breeders usually offer health guarantees to their puppy buyers covering inherited diseases.

Following are four genetic disorders that Chihuahua owners have to know about. Early detection of these conditions can save your dog's life or make him more comfortable:

COLLAPSED TRACHEA: A collapsed trachea is a common structural defect in many Toy breeds. The trachea, or windpipe, is a long tube lined with cartilage. When the cartilage is weaker than normal, external pressure (for example, a collar pulled too tightly around the neck) or internal pressure (caused by overexcitement) can damage the windpipe. Some dogs are born with softer cartilage; in others, this problem develops later in life. Persistent coughing, shortness of breath, fatigue, and a honking cough are signs of a collapsed trachea. In severe cases, fluid builds up in the lungs and shuts down the dog's airway unless the problem is treated. To prevent a collapsed trachea, use a harness when you walk your Chihuahua. Don't let him become overweight and limit strenuous exercise.

HEART MURMUR: Heart murmurs are detected in many breeds, but Chihuahuas are especially prone to this genetic disorder. A Chihuahua with this condition has a heart valve that doesn't close completely, causing the blood to backwash. The veterinarian can detect a heart murmur by listening to the heart or through cardiac ultrasound. Preventing a dog from becoming obese, providing adequate exercise, and supplying a healthy diet help protect the heart. Medication may be recommended. Murmurs sometime disappear as a dog matures, or they may remain stable without causing a health problem.

LIVER SHUNT: A liver shunt is an abnormal vessel that routes blood around the liver instead of carrying it into the liver. As a result, the dog's liver cannot do its job of filtering toxins or metabolizing nutrients carried by the blood. Puppies born with this condition will usually begin displaying symptoms as soon as they begin eating solid food. However, in

FAST FACT

It's a myth that Chihuahuas and many other toy breeds suffer adverse side effects from anesthesia. A dog undergoing surgery should be monitored during anesthesia by a trained professional monitoring the anesthesia who is dedicated to that task throughout the procedure.

Surgery may be required to treat certain serious health conditions that afflict Chihuahuas, such as patellar luxation.

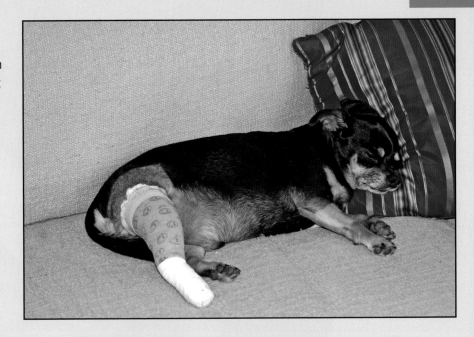

some cases symptoms may not appear until the dog is about two years old. Symptoms include poor appetite, vomiting, and diarrhea. An older dog can develop multiple shunts as a consequence of a severe liver disease, such as cirrhosis.

PATELLAR LUXATION: Patellar luxation, or slipped kneecap, affects many Toy breeds and Chihuahuas are no exception. The patella, or kneecap, is a movable flat bone at the front of the knee. When it slides out of place, it causes a dog to limp or walk bowlegged. This condition can be a congenital malformation of the knee joint or caused by an injury. It can be detected in puppies when they are six to eight weeks old, although most owners notice the problem when their puppy is between four months and a year old. The condition can range in severity, from mild cases causing little pain to severe lameness and disability. Mild cases seldom require treatment. The kneecap may pop back into place spontaneously, or your veterinarian may be able to move it back. In severe cases, surgery is the only effective treatment.

CHAPTER EIGHT

Looking Good

Grooming either a long coat or a smooth coat Chihuahua does not require a lot of time or effort. But just because Chihuahuas are a low-maintenance breed, they still need monthly bathing, weekly nail trimming, regular brushing and ear care, and daily dental care. Depending on your dog's activity level, he may require more frequent brushing or bathing.

Taking care of your dog's appearance has many benefits. Think of grooming as an investment in his overall health. Grooming sessions give you an opportunity to spot fleas, ticks, bumps, cuts, or damaged nails that may require medical attention. If

Although Chihuahuas are low-maintenance dogs, they need regular brushing to look their best.

your Chihuahua's coat starts to become thin—a sign of illness, thyroid disorder, or allergy—you'll notice it quickly when you brush him.

Grooming sessions also help with socialization. A Chihuahua that is used to being handled regularly will not be quite as skittish when he visits the veterinarian or meets a new person.

Finally, your Chihuahua will seem happier when he's clean and mat-free. It's much more pleasant to share your lap with a sweet-smelling dog that isn't scratching or irritated. Regular grooming will strengthen the bond between you and your Chihuahua.

Keeping your little dog looking his best doesn't require the attention of a professional groomer. With a few inexpensive tools, some practice, and a little patience you can easily handle the job yourself in the comfort of your own home.

ESTABLISHING A GROOMING ROUTINE

Start your Chihuahua's grooming routine the day after you bring him home. Even if your puppy is less than six months of age and doesn't seem to require much grooming, he needs to learn to accept being brushed and groomed. Chihuahuas are notorious for their tough deter-

mination to resist authority. It's important for owners to train their puppies or new adults to tolerate regular handling.

Choose a time when you can give your dog your total attention and don't have to rush. Sprucing up your dog's appearance should always be a positive experience for both of you. If you've never groomed a dog before, or if your Chihuahua is a little skittish, don't expect to perform all of the procedures the first time. Your Chihuahua will need time to adjust to being fussed over.

At the start of each grooming session, take a few minutes to give your dog a wellness check. This helps your Chihuahua tolerate general handling and will build your confidence, too. Sometimes beginning dog owners are hesitant to clip nails or give their dogs a bath. They're afraid of hurting them, especially if their Chihuahuas make a fuss or don't want to be touched. But the more people handle their dogs, the easier these procedures become.

As you prepare to groom your dog, look at his overall condition. Does he seem comfortable or stiff? Is he quieter than normal or his regular bouncy self? Run your hands over his entire body. Are there bumps, scratches, red areas, open sores, or unusual discharges? Does he wince in pain or act sensitive when you touch certain areas? If so, a visit to the veterinarian may be in order. If you see signs of fleas or ticks on his skin, take steps to get rid of them right away.

Open your Chihuahua's tiny mouth and check his teeth. If he has bad breath or his gums look red and swollen, it could be a sign of infection. Examine the insides of his ears. A strong, musty odor usually signals an ear infection. Other signs of ear infection include your dog shaking his head or rubbing it on the ground.

Make these quick checks a game. You want your Chihuahua to enjoy being handled, not dread the experience. Reassure him with gentle praise, but don't coddle your dog if he fusses. Most importantly, persist in doing what you have to do. If you back off, your Chihuahua will learn that if he protests enough, you'll stop touching him. Remain firm, but don't handle him roughly or lose your temper. When you're finished, praise him and give him a treat.

TOOLS AND EQUIPMENT

To groom a Chihuahua, you'll need the following supplies: a canine toothbrush or small fingerbrush and canine toothpaste; cotton strips; ear cleaner; a fine-toothed flea comb; nail clippers or a nail grinder; a non-slip bathmat; one or two towels and a wash cloth; and a canine blow dryer. If you have a long coat Chihuahua, you'll need a metal comb with medium- and fine-spaced teeth and a small slicker brush. For a smooth coat Chihuahua, a small bristle brush or grooming glove will do. You'll also need to find a gentle dog shampoo formulated for your Chihuahua's specific coat type (long or smooth); long coat Chihuahuas also benefit from a moisturizing conditioner. Don't forget treats to reward your dog after a grooming session.

To make brushing and nail clipping easier, you might purchase a sturdy grooming table that has a grooming arm and loop to hold him in place. Putting a Chihuahua on an elevated, nonskid surface, such as a bathroom counter or picnic table, also works. However, never leave a dog alone on any raised surface, as

FAST FACT

A special grooming tool, called a mat splitter, helps separate matted hair. For persistent mats, try spritzing on some canine detangling spray after bathing your dog. This product can also be used between baths when his coat is dry.

You'll need to spend a little extra time each day caring for your long coat Chihuahua, to make sure that he looks his best. Regular coat care will reduce the likelihood of matted fur, which can be painful to remove.

he could fall off and become badly injured.

Assemble all the grooming supplies you'll need for the session before getting started. That way, you won't have to stop in the middle and leave your dog unattended because you forgot something.

PROPER BRUSHING

Good regular brushing is the secret to a healthy and pleasant-smelling Chihuahua coat. Brushing removes dirt, loose or dead hair, and skin particles, and distributes natural oils evenly throughout the coat.

A smooth coat Chihuahua should be brushed at least twice a week with a small bristle brush or grooming glove. This collects loose hair, reduc-

ing the amount that falls on clothes and floors. Long coat Chihuahuas require daily brushing. This helps prevent mats, or clumps of fine hairs, from forming in the coat, particularly behind the elbows, ears, and tail. A slicker brush or a rubber-tipped pin brush aids can be used to help detangle the coat. Pin brushes are softer than slicker brushes and prevent hair from breaking.

To brush your dog, stand your Chihuahua on an elevated surface or lay him on your lap, right side up. Start at the base of his spine, and brush in the direction opposite the way the hairs lay. This quickly removes dead and loose hair that's ready to shed. Don't just rub the brush over the top of his coat; brush down to the skin. Then, starting at the back of the neck, brush in the reverse direction. Don't forget to brush your dog's neck, chest, and tummy as well as his back and sides. Gently use a comb to wok out any tangles. When the job is done, wipe your Chihuahua down with a damp towel. This will pick up loose hairs.

DENTAL CARE

Brushing a dog's teeth was once considered silly, but today this aspect of grooming is considered vital to your Chihuahua's health. Because of their tiny mouths and the close spacing of their teeth, Chihuahuas are prone to developing gum disease, which leads to tooth loss. By brushing your dog's teeth once a day, you can help avoid this problem.

Begin a dental regime with your dog the day after you bring him home. You can train your Chihuahua to allow a canine toothbrush or a small finger brush in his mouth. To make him comfortable with having a strange object in his mouth, put a little canine toothpaste on your finger

and rub it on his gums. Add some paste to the brush, then let him lick it off a few times. Then, gradually insert the brush and paste into his mouth and brush one or two teeth. Expand the area brushed each day until you're brushing all of his teeth.

It will take several sessions for your dog to feel comfortable with the dental procedure. Fortunately, dogs like the taste of canine toothpaste, which doesn't need to be rinsed away. Your Chihuahua should have a professional dental cleaning once every six months to a year. This can be done by your veterinarian.

EAR CLEANING

Develop the habit of checking your dog's ears for infection every few

When cleaning your Chihuahua's ears, a cotton strip or cotton ball can be used to wipe away cleaning solution, wax, and dirt. Never push a cotton swab or anything else into your dog's ear canal, as you can cause injury.

days. Healthy ears should be clean, dry, pale pink, and odorless. If you detect a foul-smelling odor, this is a sign of waxy buildup and indicates that your dog's ears need to be cleaned. For persistent ear scratching, head shaking, or if your Chihuahua is rubbing his ears on the ground, take him to the veterinarian for an examination.

To clean your dog's ears, drip a little medicated ear cleaner inside each ear opening. (Your veterinarian can suggest an over-the-counter solution.) Hold the base of his ear on the outside between your fingers and rub the ear together a few times. This loosens the debris. Insert a cotton strip inside the ear as far as possible before twisting and turning it to wipe out the debris. Repeat the process until a new piece of cotton comes out clean and dry. Since the canine inner ear is a long L-shaped canal, you can safely clean it without hurting your dog.

NAIL CLIPPING

Long nails on a Chihuahua can cause many problems. It's difficult for a dog to walk if his nails are in the way. Your Chihuahua should be able to stand on the floor and not have his nails hit the ground. When nails grow too long they can easily catch on clothing or furniture and tear or

FAST FACT

Sage can be used to help treat gingivitis. If your dog's gums are inflamed, add 1/2 teaspoon of crumbled sage leaves to his food once a day. You can also make a sage tea for your dog by pouring 2 cups of boiling water over 2 teaspoons of chopped fresh sage (or 1 teaspoon of dried sage). Let this mixture stand for 15 minutes, then refrigerate, and serve to your Chihuahua when chilled.

fracture the bone inside the nail. Bleeding nails are painful and may require an emergency trip to the veterinarian. Proper care includes trimming your Chihuahua's nails at least once a week to keep them from growing too long.

To trim your dog's nails use dog nail clippers or an electric nail grinder. Here's where a helper comes in handy. Place your dog on top of a nonslip surface or between the helper's knees, facing outward, with a hand supporting the dog's chest. Gently lift one of his dog's paws. Holding it firmly between your thumb and fingers, clip off the white tip at the end of one of the nails. Praise your dog if he behaves nicely and tell him, "No" if he fusses.

Only trim his nails back a little bit at a time. If you cut the nail too

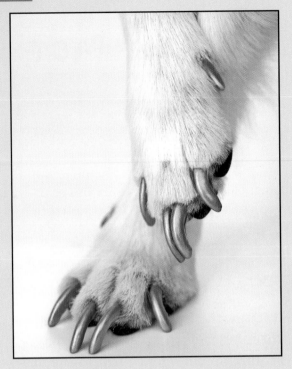

Your Chihuahua will accept nail clipping more easily if you handle his paws several times a day. Get in the habit of picking him up and gently running your fingers around the pads of his feet and toenails. When done, praise your dog for letting you handle his feet.

BATHING YOUR BEAUTY

Bathing your Chihuahua improves the quality of his coat and gives your dog a nice odor, making him a pleasure to have around. You can bathe your Chihuahua every two weeks to a month; more frequent shampooing can irritate his sensitive skin. Use a gentle doggy shampoo with a pH level of 4.5 to 5.5; shampoo made for people is too harsh for your dog's sensitive skin.

You can bathe your Chihuahua in a kitchen sink, or in a bathtub with a rubber non-skid mat. Gather all

far back, you'll hit the quick, the nail's blood supply. This will cause bleeding and pain. On dogs with translucent nails, the quick appears to be a dark line running through the nail. It hard to see in dogs with dark nails, so be careful. As you become more experienced, you'll develop a better idea of how much you can cut your Chihuahua's nails.

If you do hit the quick, don't panic. Just apply pressure with a wet washcloth or dab on an anticoagulant, such as styptic powder or cornstarch, to stop the bleeding.

If you're not comfortable clipping your dog's nails, take him to a professional groomer or to your veterinarian to get the job done.

When a dog walks on concrete or other hard surfaces, it can help to keep his nails short. However, the rate at which a dog's nails grow depends both on their genetic makeup and on how much protein they consume.

bathing supplies before putting your dog in the sink or tub, and never leave your dog unattended, as he may try to jump out and hurt himself.

A spray hose attachment makes the job easier. Use this to wet your dog's coat with warm water. Once his coat is wet, pour a little shampoo on a washcloth or a rubber brush and rub it into your dog's coat. After he's thoroughly lathered, rinse the soap out of his coat. Any soap that remains will create a sticky residue, attracting dirt and grime, so make sure that it's all washed away. If you have a long coat Chihuahua, you may next want to use a canine conditioner on his coat. Again, make sure you rinse it out completely. Finally, wet your dog's head, rub in shampoo, and rinse it out. Be particularly careful not to get water into your dog's ears.

When the bath is done, wrap a towel around your Chihuahua to prevent him from getting a chill and rub him vigorously until he's dry. For a long coat Chihuahua, using a canine hair dryer will help keep his hair from getting tangled. As you dry, brush his coat in the same direction as it grows.

COAT TRIMMING

Unlike some other dogs in the Toy Group, the Chihuahua doesn't

When bathing your Chihuahua, try to wash and rinse his coat without getting his head wet. Once your Chihuahua's head gets wet, he'll want to shake off the water, soaking you in the process.

require a lot of fancy trimming and clipping. Unless you have a show dog and plan to enter him in conformation events, trimming is optional. Sure it will make him look a little tidier, but there's no healthy reason to do it. Besides, trimming for the show ring requires expertise and practice.

If you want to trim your long coat Chihuahua, you'll need a professional-grade pair of thinning shears. Start by trimming the hair around the base of his tail to keep that area clean. Trim off any long hair on his legs and around the bottoms of your dog's feet, but don't trim between the pads. His delicate feet need that extra cushion. Clip off long hairs on the toes that extend past the nails; this fringe of hair should have a slightly oval appearance. Watch what you're doing as you trim. Otherwise, it's easy to shear off more coat than you want. Your Chihuahua should have a natural appearance, rather than a finely sculpted look.

Some smooth coat Chihuahuas have thicker coats with extra fringe along the dog's neck, backs of the thighs, behind the ears, and belly. You can carefully trim these areas flat to create a neater outline, but don't shave your dog. He needs this protection for warmth.

If you don't feel comfortable trimming your Chihuahua's coat, a professional groomer can perform this job. However, make sure to give this person explicit instructions about what you expect. Otherwise, your long coat Chihuahua could end up looking like a smooth coat Chihuahua!

CHAPTER NINE

Getting Out With Your Chihuahua

Chihuahuas need regular outings to maintain peak physical and mental health. Dogs that sleep around the house all day are likely to gain weight and develop joint strain or torn ligaments. Inactivity also brings on boredom and behavior issues, such as barking and destructive chewing.

Puppies exercise naturally, but as they grow older they will lose interest in running around the house. You'll have to make sure that your Chihuahua gets enough daily exercise. A 20-minute walk in the morning, and another in the evening, will be plenty. You can mix things up by letting your dog run off-leash in a

Daily opportunities to exercise outdoors will help maintain your Chihuahua's good health.

fenced yard or safe open area. Play a game of fetch, or see if you can get him to push a soccer ball around. Any activity that gets your Chihuahua moving around will make him healthy and happy.

Don't take your Chihuahua out for exercise right after he eats. Be aware of the temperature: don't let him overdo it on hot afternoons, and dress him in a sweater on cool mornings. When he's done exercising, make sure your Chihuahua has access to plenty of fresh water.

ACTIVITIES FOR YOUR CHIHUAHUA

Getting your dog involved in canine sports helps timid Chihuahuas to build their confidence and teaches hyperactive dogs to manage their impulses. Chihuahuas are great athletes that are quite capable of taking on physical challenges. These small dogs can do well in such organized sports as agility, flyball, canine musical freestyle, competitive obedience, and rally.

AGILITY: Chihuahuas are easily capable of performing the leaps and bounds required to succeed in agility competitions. In agility, handler and dog work as a team to complete a series of complex maneuvers on an obstacle course as quickly as possible. The owner guides the dog to run through tunnels, jump over hurdles, walk over a teeter-totter, scale an A-frame, and navigate weave poles and balance beams. This fast-paced

Curious Chihuahuas tend to stick their faces into everything while walking outdoors. As a result, their protruding eyes become a magnet for seed particles, dust, dirt, pollen, and other foreign objects. Besides contributing to allergies, the debris can irritate or damage the cornea. To avoid eye injuries after outdoor exercise, flush your dog's eyes with veterinary artificial tears or sterile saline solution.

Chihuahuas can compete successfully in AKC agility events. The courses are adjusted depending on the size of the dog. Most Chihuahuas have no problem clearing the eight-inch (20 cm) jumps that are standard for their group, which can include Corgies and small Shelties.

canine sport lets active Chihuahuas use their thinking skills.

FLYBALL: Chihuahuas love flyball and can excel at this fast-paced sport. Dogs compete as part of a four-member relay team. Each dog takes a turn sprinting down a 51-foot lane, leaping over four hurdles spaced 10 feet apart. The hurdle heights depend on the size of the smallest dog on the team. After completing the hurdles, the dog steps on a spring-loaded box that shoots out a tennis ball. The dog catches the tennis ball and returns to the starting point, jumping the four hurdles again on the way. The North American Flyball Association sponsors competitions.

CANINE MUSICAL FREESTYLE: If you've ever wanted to dance with your Chihuahua, consider training him for canine musical freestyle. In this fun sport, dog and handler perform a choreographed routine set to music. Dance steps incorporate basic obedience commands, known as heelwork, such as "sit," "down," and "front." Routines include creative moves featuring pivots, kicks, twists, and turns. You and your dog can do this at home for your own amusement or you can perform for cheering onlookers at competitive events. The Canine Freestyle Federation (CFF) and the World Canine Freestyle Organization (WCFO) sponsor competitions in the United States.

Intelligent, sure-footed Chihuahuas are fast learners. They pick up the steps by watching their handlers' body language and listening to the instructions. They also won't mind wearing the simple costumes that are required.

Musical freestyle events give your dog an opportunity to entertain others.

OBEDIENCE: When Chihuahuas compete in obedience contests, they master the valuable ability to respond to commands. Training for these events is good opportunity for dog and owner to strengthen their bond and learn how to understand each other's body language.

In competitive obedience, dogs begin with a perfect score of 200 points. A judge deducts points each time a dog fails to perform an exercise correctly. To earn the basic obedience title of Companion Dog (CD), dogs must earn a leg—scoring at least 170 points in a single trial, plus at least 50 percent of the points in each individual exercise—at three different trials. Advanced titles include Companion Dog Excellent (CDX), Utility Dog (UD), Utility Dog Excellent (UDX), and the highest title, Obedience Trial Champion (OTCH).

AKC Rally: If you're looking for a dog sport with less regimentation than obedience, and not as much activity as agility, AKC Rally might be right up your alley. In this organized recreation program, you and your Chihuahua complete a course of 10 to 20 stations chosen by the Rally judge. A sign at each station gives instructions to the dog and handler team to follow basic obedience skills, such as sit, heel in a figure-8 pattern, or lie down. Owners can talk, clap their hands, or whistle to their dogs during the competition. At the novice level, dogs remain on their leash. At advanced or excellent levels, the dogs complete the stations while off-leash.

With a little training, Chihuahuas can participate in AKC Rally. In Rally events, dogs perform obedience exercises while on leash alongside their handlers.

SHOWING YOUR CHIHUAHUA

Any AKC-registered Chihuahua can participate in a conformation show. To succeed, you'll need a well-bred, AKC-registered Chihuahua that exudes personality. Dog shows were originally held to choose breeding stock, so entrants cannot be spayed or neutered.

If you think you would like to show your dog, carefully evaluate his chances of becoming a champion. Read the Chihuahua breed standard to see how closely your dog matches the description of the ideal Chihuahua. Attend a few dog shows to get some idea of the training required and the procedures you'll need to master for showing.

It helps if you bought your dog from a breeder who shows his or her Chihuahuas. This person will be able to evaluate your dog's chances and can help you get started in this sport.

FAST FACT

Smooth coat and long coat Chihuahuas are judged separately in the conformation ring, although the Chihuahua breed standard applies to both types of dog.

Most champion Chihuahuas come from a long line of champions.

THERAPY WORK

The Chihuahua's lively personality, affectionate nature, and willingness to learn make him the ideal four-footed therapist. His small size is another plus, as he'll take up little room on a patient's lap in a wheelchair or lying beside someone who is bedridden. Chihuahuas who are trained for pet therapy provide comfort and joy to patients in hospitals, nursing homes, and other facilities. Often trained Chihuahuas entertain by performing tricks and wearing fun costumes.

Therapy dogs must be bathed and brushed before showing up for work. Many Chihuahuas also require advanced training before they can work in a therapeutic setting. Therapy dogs are certified by organizations like Therapy Dogs International (www.tdi-dog.org) or the Delta Society (www.deltasociety.org).

Chihuahuas make excellent certified hearing dogs. These working dogs open the lines of communication between their owners and the hearing world. They alert their owners to sounds in the home, such as the phone, doorbell or smoke alarm, and sounds outside the home, such as a car or person coming up behind them, or someone trying to get their attention. For more information about training requirements, contact Dogs for the Deaf (www.dogs-forthedeaf.org).

TRAVELING WITH YOUR CHIHUAHUA

Chihuahuas make great traveling companions, and many people enjoy taking their portable dogs along with them on day trips or vacations. Your Chihuahua will probably be ready, willing, and able to travel wherever you go, so long as you've planned ahead for his safety and comfort.

Before you decide to take your Chihuahua touring, consider his personality, the travel challenges involved, and what you'll be doing on this outing. A dog that's used to joining you on daily errands or short overnight visits will take a longer road trip or an airplane ride in stride. The Chihuahua that's primarily a homebody may find the same journey stressful. He may shake, whine,

Some Chihuahuas can provide a useful service as assistance dogs.

TRAVEL FIRST-AID KIT

If you plan to travel with your dog, even locally, keep a canine first-aid kit in the car. Supplies to deal with emergencies should be kept in a container that closes tightly. Include the following items:

- a canine first-aid manual
- emergency contact information for your veterinarian and the pet emergency clinic
- phone number for the Animal Poison Control Center (888) 426-4435
- antibiotic ointment, antiseptic and antibacterial cleansing wipes or solution
- Benadryl
- insect repellant
- cotton-tipped applicators
- ear cleaner
- sterile gauze pads
- human or canine sunscreen
- hydrogen peroxide
- instant hot and cold packs
- towels and blankets
- latex gloves
- oral glucose solution to prevent dehydration
- lubricating jelly
- a medicine dropper
- nail clippers
- self-adhering bandages
- nonprescription medications for vomiting and diarrhea (ask your veterinarian about the type and correct dosage for your Chihuahua)
- a small notebook and pen
- small scissors
- a soft muzzle
- sterile saline eyewash
- a thermometer
- small flashlight
- a few plastic bags
- tweezers

Check the first-aid kit occasionally, and replace items that have passed their expiration dates.

or bark, or possibly suffer from motion sickness, vomiting, or diarrhea. If you're unable to cater to your dog's needs during your travels, he may be better off staying at home with a dog sitter or going to a boarding facility where you won't have to worry about him.

To introduce your dog to the travel experience, start taking her on short car rides, lasting 10 or 20 minutes. Make the experience fun, so your Chihuahua looks forward to going for a drive. If the only time your dog goes anywhere is to visit the veterinarian, she's going to hate getting in the car. So even if you don't plan on traveling with her, take her on errands with you.

Keep your Chihuahua safe when going mobile. On every car trip your dog should ride in a travel crate or be locked into a securely fastened restraint system. An unsecured dog can be a distraction, and if you're in an accident he could be badly hurt by slamming into the back of a seat or the windshield, or flying out of the vehicle. On longer trips, plan stops every two or three hours so your Chihuahua can stretch, sniff around, and go to the bathroom.

Never leave your dog in a car when it's warm! On a 73° Fahrenheit (23° Celsius) day, the temperature inside a closed car can reach 120°F (49°C) in 30 minutes. On a 90°F (32°C) day, the temperature can reach 160°F (71°C) in less than 15 minutes. High temperatures will

Make sure your Chihuahua is properly restrained any time you take him for a ride in the car. He can ride in his crate or in a soft pet carrier. There is a variety of harnesses available that can be used to secure him safely in the back seat.

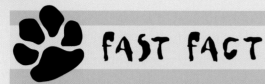

FAST FACT

To avoid motion sickness, don't feed your dog for at least an hour before you leave the house. About a half-hour before you depart, give your dog a teaspoons of honey, some Nutri Cal, or a few gingersnap cookies to settle his stomach. When driving, open the vehicle windows a little to help fresh air circulate.

cause heatstroke, which can kill your Chihuahua.

Flying with your Chihuahua will require some preparation on your part. Every airline has different policies when it comes to canine passengers. Some airlines will allow you to take a small dog with you in the plane's cabin, so long as he's in an approved pet carrier. Expect to pay a fee for this service. Others make dogs ride in an area that is separate from human passengers. The airline may have special guidelines about the size of your dog's crate. It may also require you to provide copies of paperwork showing that he is properly licensed and up-to-date on his vaccinations. Check with the airline you'll be using before it is time to leave so that you don't have any last-minute problems or expenses.

When traveling, plan your

overnight accommodations in advance. According to the American Hotel and Lodging Association, only 35 percent of all hotels welcome pets. Hotels and resorts that accommodate dog owners can be found online at PetsWelcome.com, PetTravel.com, LetsGoPets.com, and other Web sites. When you enter a hotel room, check the floor—especially beneath the bed—before letting your Chihuahua roam free. Small objects left behind by a previous guest can hurt your Chihuahua if he finds and swallows them.

LEAVING YOUR CHIHUAHUA AT HOME

Sometimes you'll need to leave your dog pal behind when you go out of town. If you're called to another city for business, your Chihuahua won't be happy staying in the hotel room all day. He'll probably bark or

FAST FACT

When you walk through airport security, you'll need to remove your dog from his crate so it can be inspected. For his safety, make sure his identification tag is securely fastened to his collar and keep his leash or harness in your purse or carry-on bag.

become destructive. If you're visiting friends or family that have other dogs, your Chihuahua might feel threatened and uncomfortable. When you can't take your Chihuahua along, you'll need to make arrangements for his care. A friend or family member might be able to look after your dog. If not, you could hire a professional dog sitter to watch your Chihuahua. Before doing this, it's always a good idea to get recommendations and interview candidates.

Other options include boarding kennels and doggie day care centers. These facilities will care for your dog, exercise him, groom him, and play with him while you are away. The best facilities have a veterinarian on staff to help with medical problems.

You can find boarding kennels and doggie day care centers in your area by using the phone book or the Internet. Your veterinarian as well as dog-owning family members and friends might also be able to give you recommendations. After finding a suitable option, you might want to tour the facility to see where your dog will be staying. The kennel or center you choose should be clean, safe, and large enough to accommodate your dog. There should also be separate areas for animals that are sick or aggressive. If the facility does not measure up to your standards, trust your instincts and look for another boarding option for your dog.

CHAPTER TEN

Caring for Your Senior Chihuahua

Chihuahuas age gracefully. Gray hairs in his muzzle and encircling his eyes give him a wise and grizzled expression. The highly energetic puppy gives way to a mellow older fellow. Around the time a Chihuahua reaches 10 years old he'll begin to slow down, but good care will help him enjoy his remaining years.

Nutritious meals, regular exercise, and mental stimulation helps slow the aging process.

Older Chihuahuas need a little more TLC than they once did. Now's the time to splurge on your dog's bedding. Memory foam and egg-crate foam dog cushions help cushion stiff joints. Keep your

Chihuahuas tend to live 15 years or more—longer than most dog breeds.

Chihuahua's sleeping area warm, and consider setting up a few more cozy napping stations around the house for him. If your dog begins slipping on the floor, place nonskid rubber mats around the house. Putting up baby gates will help prevent him from wandering out of open doors or falling down stairs.

Since potty accidents become more frequent as your dog ages, take him outdoors often and get used to the idea of mopping up. A senior Chihuahua can't help his loss of bladder control.

Don't hesitate to take him to the veterinarian if you notice any radical changes in his condition.

NUTRITION

Ideally, your senior Chihuahua should not gain weight. Extra weight makes the heart and other vital organs work harder, and adds stress to joint cartilage and ligaments. These things can shorten your dog's life. As your older Chihuahua becomes less active, you can reduce the size of his meals to compensate. If your dog does become overweight, cut down on his portion, add more steamed or finely diced vegetables to his meals, and increase his exercise periods.

Some older dogs look forward to their meals, while others have a diminished sense of smell or taste and pick at their food. IF that's the case with your Chihuahua, vary the ingredients to make dinnertime more interesting. Try adding some new flavors to entice him, such as fish or liver. Consider adding essential fatty acids, in the form of fish oil, to prevent him from developing dry skin. Diets rich in antioxidants such as vitamin E, lutein, and beta-carotene can improve a dog's immunity and delay some problems of old age.

EXERCISE

As they age, senior Chihuahuas begin to develop stiff joints and have trouble moving around. To keep your dog as mobile as possible, encourage him to go with you on short, daily walks. These will help him maintain muscle mass, joint flexibility, and bone density.

FAST FACT

Reverse sneezing sounds scary, but it's not an emergency. When a senior Chihuahua gets too excited, eats or drinks too quickly, or pulls on his leash, he may start snorting, honking, or wheezing. Distract your dog by gently rubbing his throat. This will induce him to swallow.

Daily outings can also help improve your dog's mental state by improving oxygen flow to his brain. Smelling the flowers outdoors, walking on different surfaces, and feeling the breeze will keep an older dog interested in life.

If your senior Chihuahua is in good health, consider entering him in a rally competition. This sport provides interaction with other dogs and helps break up the routine. It's perfect for senior dogs who no longer show in obedience but are still willing to work.

SENIOR HEALTH PROBLEMS

Aches and pains are just part of the aging process. As Chihuahuas advance in years, they're prone to other problems as well, such as incontinence, hearing loss, and blindness. While these problems can be disheartening to see and deal with, they won't shorten your dog's life. Other common old-age problems that can have more of an effect are kidney disease, osteoarthritis, and cancer.

Don't expect your Chihuahua to express signs of suffering. That's because dogs only exhibit a small portion of the pain they are really experiencing. Like their ancestors in the wild, showing pain or illness makes them too vulnerable to predators.

Finding common medical issues sooner rather than later enables you

SENIOR DENTAL ISSUES

As dogs age, they develop dental issues and often lose teeth. This can make eating dry dog food difficult. Soaking your dog's kibble in warm water for several minutes, and mixing in some moist canned food can help with this problem.

When your dog is a senior, maintaining good oral health becomes even more important. Feeding your Chihuahua some grated, finely chopped, or steamed pieces of fresh fruits and vegetables can help keep his teeth clean. Allowing him to chew on raw bones can also help scrape plaque and tartar off his teeth. You can ask a local butcher to cut up raw marrowbones for your Chihuahua, but make sure they're too big for him to swallow. Finally, brush his teeth once or even twice a day, and take him to the veterinarian every six months for a professional cleaning.

Even as your Chihuahua ages, he'll still enjoy spending time with you.

to provide treatment for your Chihuahua and help him live more comfortably. Once your dog turns eight years old he should have a senior wellness checkup every six months. During the visit the veterinarian will perform blood tests and laboratory procedures to check your Chihuahua's kidney and liver functions. These screening exams can also detect heart disease, adrenal disorders, or cancer. When caught early, treatment may add years to your dog's life.

SAYING GOOD-BYE

It is a sad fact that dogs live shorter lifespans than humans. Eventually, you'll have to live without your beloved canine companion. Some dogs will die peacefully in their sleep at a ripe old age. In other cases, such as when your Chihuahua has a debilitating, incurable illness that is causing him constant pain, you may have to decide when he takes his last breath.

The decision to end a dog's life is the most difficult part of dog owner-

It is common for a Chihuahua's dark hair to begin showing signs of gray as he ages, particularly around his face and muzzle.

ship, but remember that your Chihuahua has always relied on you to care for him to the best of your ability. When making this end-of-life decision, consider the quality of your dog's life. Ask yourself what five activities did your Chihuahua love doing above all else while he was still healthy and active. If he's no longer able to do any of these things, the time may have come to say good-bye.

As the last days approach, give family members and friends a chance to say good-bye to him. You could have a party, allowing people to share their favorite memories and thank your Chihuahua for all the pleasure he's provided. Or, take your Chihuahua for a picnic at a favorite spot and have a friend photograph you and your dog together there.

The word *euthanasia* comes from a Greek term meaning "good death."

FAST FACT

Veterinary researchers estimate that a dog's life span is 25 percent determined by his genes and 75 percent dependent on environmental factors.

The actual process is painless for your dog. The veterinarian will usually administer a sedative first, so your friend will fall asleep. Then an overdose of anesthesia is administered, and the dog's heart simply stops beating.

Give yourself as much time to grieve as you need. There's no time limit to missing your longtime canine companion. When you feel ready, you may want to share your life with another Chihuahua again. A special puppy is waiting for you to take him home.

Organizations to Contact

American Animal Hospital Association
12575 West Bayaud Ave.
Lakewood, CO 80228
Phone: 303-986-2800
Fax: 800-252-2242
E-mail: info@aahanet.org
Web site: www.aahanet.org

American Canine Association, Inc.
P.O. Box 808
Phoenixville, PA 19460
Phone: 800-651-8332
Fax: 800-422-1864
E-mail: acacanines@aol.com
Web site: www.acainfo.com

American Dog Breeders Assn.
P.O. Box 1771
Salt Lake City, UT 84110
Phone: 801-936-7513
E-mail: bstofshw@adba.cc
Web site: www.adbadogs.com

American Humane Association
63 Inverness Dr. East
Englewood, CO 80112
Phone: 303-792-9900
Fax: 303-792-5333
Web site: www.americanhumane.org

American Kennel Club
8051 Arco Corporate Dr., Suite 100
Raleigh, NC 27617
Phone: 919-233-9767
E-mail: info@akc.org
Web site: www.akc.org

Association of Pet Dog Trainers
150 Executive Center Dr., Box 35
Greenville, SC 29615
Phone: 800-738-3647
E-mail: information@apdt.com
Web site: www.apdt.com

The British Chihuahua Club
Hon. Secretary Mr. Guy Hazlehurst
14 Stonefield Park
Maidenhead, Berks SL6 6ES
United Kingdom
Web site: www.the-british-chihuahua-club.org.uk

The Canadian Kennel Club
89 Skyway Avenue, Suite 100
Etobicoke, Ontario, M9W 6R4
Canada
Phone: 416-675-5511
Fax: 416-675-6506
E-mail: information@ckc.ca
Web site: www.ckc.ca/en

**Canine Eye Registration
Foundation**
1717 Philo Road
P.O. Box 3007
Urbana, IL 61803-3007
Phone: 217-693-4800
Fax: 217-693-4801
E-mail: cerf@vmdb.org
Web site: www.vmdb.org/cerf.html

**Canine Health
Foundation**
P.O. Box 37941
Raleigh, NC 27627-7941
Phone: 888-682-9696
Fax: 919-334-4011
E-mail: akcchf@akc.org
Web site: www.akcchf.org

Chihuahua Club of America, Inc.
Patricia Larrissey, Secretary
11430 Clifton Blvd Apt. 207
Cleveland OH 44102
E-mail: larcey@att.net
Web site: www.chihuahuaclub
    ofamerica.com

Chihuahua Club of Canada
2114 Dublin St.
New Westminster
Province BC V3M 3A9
Canada
Phone: 604-521-0922
Web site: www.canadogs.com

Delta Society
875 124th Ave., NE
Suite 101
Bellevue, WA 98005
Phone: 425-226-7357
E-mail: info@deltasociety.org
Web site: www.deltasociety.org

**Humane Society
of the United States**
2100 L St., NW
Washington, DC 20037
Phone: 202-452-1100
Fax: 301-548-7701
E-mail: info@hsus.org
Web site: www.hsus.org

**The Kennel Club
of the United Kingdom**
1-5 Clarges St.
Picadilly, London W1J 8AB
United Kingdom
Phone: 0870 606 6750
Fax: 020 7518 1058
Web site: www.thekennelclub.org.uk

**National Association of Dog
Obedience Instructors**
PMB 369
729 Grapevine Hwy
Hurst, TX 76054-2085
E-mail: corrsec2@nadoi.org
Web site: www.nadoi.org

**National Association of
Professional Pet Sitters (NAPPS)**
17000 Commerce Parkway, Suite C
Mt. Laurel, NJ 08054
Phone: 856-439-0324
Fax: 856-439-0525
E-mail: napps@ahint.com
Web site: www.petsitters.org

National Dog Registry
P.O. Box 51105
Mesa, AZ 85208
Phone: 800-NDR-DOGS
E-mail: info@nationaldogregistry.com
Web site: www.nationaldogregistry.com

**North American Dog Agility
Council (NADAC)**
P.O. Box 1206
Colbert, OK 74733
E-mail: info@nadac.com
Web site: www.nadac.com

**North American Flyball
Association (NAFA)**
1400 West Devon Ave., #512
Chicago, IL 60660
Phone: 800-318-6312
E-mail: flyball@flyball.org
Web site: www.flyball.org

**Orthopedic Foundation
for Animals (OFA)**
2300 East Nifong Boulevard
Columbia, MO 65201
Phone: 573-442-0418
Fax: 573-875-5073
Web site: www.offa.org

Pet Industry Joint Advisory Council
1220 19th Street, NW Suite 400
Washington, DC 20036
Phone: 202-452-1525
Fax: 202-293-4377
E-mail: info@pijac.org
Web site: www.pijac.org

Pet Loss Support Hotline
College of Veterinary Medicine
Cornell University
Ithaca, NY 14853-6401
Phone: 607-253-3932
Web site: www.vet.cornell.edu/
public/petloss

Pet Sitters International (PSI)
201 East King Street
King, NC 27021-9161
Phone: 336-983-9222
Fax: 336-983-9222
E-mail: info@petsit.com
Web site: www.petsit.com

Therapy Dogs International, Inc.
88 Bartley Road
Flanders, NJ 07836
Phone: 973-252-9800
Web site: www.tdi-dog.org

UK National Pet Register
74 North Albert Street, Dept 2
Fleetwood, Lancasterhire, FY7 6BJ
United Kingdom
Web site: www.nationalpetregister.org

**United States Dog Agility
Association, Inc. (USDAA)**
P.O. Box 850955
Richardson, TX 75085-0955
Phone: 972-487-2200
Fax: 972-272-4404
Web site: www.usdaa.com

Veterinary Medical Databases
1717 Philo Rd.
PO Box 3007
Urbana, IL 61803-3007
Phone: 217-693-4800
E-mail: cerf@vmdb.org
Web site: www.vmdb.org

**World Canine Freestyle
Organization (WCFO)**
PO Box 350122
Brooklyn, NY 11235-2525
Phone: 718-332-8336
E-mail: wcfodogs@aol.com
Web site: www.worldcaninefreestyle.org

Further Reading

Clothier, Suzanne. *Bones Would Rain from the Sky: Deepening Our Relationships With Dogs*. New York: Grand Central Publishing, 2005.

Coile, Caroline. *The Chihuahua Handbook*. Hauppauge, N.Y.: Barron's Educational Series, 2010.

Eldredge, Debra. *Dog Owner's Veterinary Handbook*. New York: Howell Book House, 2007.

Fernandez, Amy. *Barron's Dog Bibles: Chihuahuas*. Hauppauge, N.Y.: Barron's Educational Series, 2009.

Gagne, Tammy. *The Chihuahua*. Neptune City, N.J.: TFH Publications, 2005.

Gewirtz, Elaine Waldorf, with Jordan Herod Nucciom, DVM, CVA. *The Everything Natural Health Book For Dogs*. Avon, Mass.: Adams Media, 2009.

Gewirtz, Elaine. *Fetch This Book! Train Your Dog to Do Almost Anything*. Pittsburgh: Eldorado Ink, 2010.

———. *Your Happy Healthy Pet Chihuahua*. 2nd ed. Hoboken, N.J.: Wiley Publishing, 2006.

McConnell, Patricia. *For the Love of a Dog: Understanding Emotion in You and Your Best Friend*. New York: Ballantine Books, 2007.

Miller, Pat. *The Power of Positive Dog Training*. Hoboken, N.J.: Wiley Publishing, 2008.

O'Neill, Jacqueline. *Chihuahuas for Dummies*. Hoboken, N.J.: Wiley Publishing, 2001.

Palika, Liz. *The Ultimate Pet Food Guide: Everything You Need to Know About Feeding Your Dog or Cat*. Cambridge, Mass.: Da Capo Press, 2008.

Schade, Victoria. *Bonding with Your Dog*. Hoboken, N.J.: Wiley Publishing, 2009.

Internet Resources

www.avsabonline.org

The Web site of the American Veterinary Society of Animal Behavior (AVSAB), a group of veterinarians and research professionals post position statements on behavior issues.

www.aspca.org/pet-care/poison-control/

The American Society for the Prevention of Cruelty to Animals (ASPCA) has a poison control center Web page that is the best resource for poison-related animal emergencies.

www.avma.org

The American Veterinary Medical Association's Web site offers a wide range of medical information for dog owners.

www.chihuahuaclubofamerica.com

Chihuahua fanciers can learn more about the breed's behavior, care, health and training from the Chihuahua Club of America's Web site.

www.healthypet.com

The American Animal Hospital Association (AAHA) accredits veterinary hospitals and clinics throughout the United States and Canada.

Publisher's Note: The Web sites listed on these pages were active at the time of publication. The publisher is not responsible for Web sites that have changed their address or discontinued operation since the date of publication.

www.vetmed.wsu.edu

The Washington State University of College of Veterinary Medicine Web site covers a wide range of pet health topics.

www.akc.org/breeds/chihuahua/index.cfm

You will find the American Kennel Club's breed standard for the Chihuahua at this site.

www.thekennelclub.org.uk/item/183

The Kennel Club of the United Kingdom posts its breed standard for the smooth coat Chihuahua at this site.

http://clickertraining.com

Karen Pryor Clicker Training is an educational resource with information and how-to tips about clicker training, a form of operant conditioning that is both effective and enjoyable.

www.westminsterkennelclub.org

This website includes breed information, showmanship videos, and details about the Westminster Dog Show.

Index

Numbers in **bold italics** refer to captions.

Contributors

ELAINE WALDORF GEWIRTZ, a lifelong dog owner and trainer, is the author of nearly two dozen books and nearly a hundred magazine articles. She's a multiple recipient of the prestigious Maxwell Award for writing excellence from the Dog Writers' Association of America. Her books and articles have earned the ASPCA Humane Issues, Eukanuba, and Wiley/Ellsworth S. Howell Awards.

Senior Consulting Editor **GARY KORSGAARD, DVM,** has had a long and distinguished career in veterinary medicine. After graduating from The Ohio State University's College of Veterinary Medicine in 1963, he spent two years as a captain in the Veterinary Corps of the U.S. Army. During that time he attended the Walter Reed Army Institute of Research and became Chief of the Veterinary Division for the Sixth Army Medical Laboratory at the Presidio, San Francisco.

In 1968 Dr. Korsgaard founded the Monte Vista Veterinary Hospital in Concord, California, where he practiced for 32 years as a small animal veterinarian. He is a past president of the Contra Costa Veterinary Association, and was one of the founding members of the Contra Costa Veterinary Emergency Clinic, serving as president and board member of that hospital for nearly 30 years.

Dr. Korsgaard retired in 2000. He enjoys golf, hiking, international travel, and spending time with his wife Susan and their three children and four grandchildren.